NOTHING IS WRONG
AND HERE IS WHY

ALSO BY ALEXANDRA PETRI

A Field Guide to Awkward Silences

NOTHING IS WRONG AND HERE IS WHY

Essays

ALEXANDRA PETRI

W. W. NORTON & COMPANY
Independent Publishers Since 1923

Pieces that appeared previously in the *Washington Post* are followed
by their original publication date.

Copyright © 2020 by Alexandra Petri

For information about permission to reproduce selections from this
book, write to Permissions, W. W. Norton & Company, Inc.,
500 Fifth Avenue, New York, NY 10110

For information about special discounts for bulk purchases, please
contact W. W. Norton Special Sales at specialsales@wwnorton.com
or 800-233-4830

Manufacturing by Lake Book Manufacturing
Book design by Lovedog Studio
Production manager: Lauren Abbate

Library of Congress Cataloging-in-Publication Data

Names: Petri, Alexandra, author.
Title: Nothing is wrong and here is why : essays / Alexandra Petri.
Description: First edition. | New York : W. W. Norton & Company, 2020.
Identifiers: LCCN 2020007461 | ISBN 9781324006459 (hardcover) |
ISBN 9781324006466 (epub)
Subjects: LCSH: Trump, Donald, 1946– —Humor. | Presidents—United
States—Humor. | United States—Politics and government—2017– —Humor.
Classification: LCC E913.3 .P48 2020 | DDC 973.933092—dc23
LC record available at https://lccn.loc.gov/2020007461

W. W. Norton & Company, Inc., 500 Fifth Avenue, New York, N.Y. 10110
www.wwnorton.com

W. W. Norton & Company Ltd., 15 Carlisle Street, London W1D 3BS

1 2 3 4 5 6 7 8 9 0

To Steve
You are a good man and I like you
(sorry, I panicked)

Contents

Introduction   XV

Prologue: Welcome to the New Physics!   1

Part I
The Brightest Timeline

Chris Christie's Wordless Screaming   5

Waiting for Pivot: A GOP Tragicomedy   8

Nasty Women   15

Donald Trump and His Sons Will Never
Talk Business Again   18

The True, Correct Story of What Happened
at Donald Trump's Inauguration   23

Trump's Budget Makes Perfect Sense and
Will Fix America, and I Will Tell You Why   27

Every Story I Have Read About Trump
Supporters in the Past Week   32

This Is Not a Crisis, Republicans Say, as a
Large Spider Slowly Devours Them   35

What the Ethics Chief Really Wanted to Say
in His Resignation Letter   38

A Moderate Speaks: By God, Won't Someone
Else Take a Stand?   42

How Paul Manafort Came by $934,350 in
Antique Carpets   45

Melania Trump Wants to Spend Christmas on
a Deserted Island (With Her Family)   49

The Day Donald Trump First Became a
Stable Genius   52

Welcome to the Normal, Low-End Furniture Store
for Trump Cabinet Members   57

Keep Scott Pruitt Moist   61

I'm Beginning to Suspect These Were Not, in Fact,
the Best People   64

HOW DARE YOU DO THIS TO
BRETT KAVANAUGH?   67

The FBI Has Been Very Easy to Reach about Brett Kavanaugh,
and Of Course the Report Has Been Quite Easy to Read   70

You Are in Melania Trump's Nightmare Forest of
Cursed Red Trees. Keep to the Path.   75

Lock Her Up?   78

My Book Report on *The Mueller Report*   81

You Think Trump's Getting Impeached? I Defy You
to Convince Anyone at This Cursed Truck Stop.   85

Part II

ROUTINE NIGHTMARES
AND SOOTHING FABLES

It Is Very Difficult to Get the Train to Stop   91

A Humanizing Profile of Your Local Neo-Nazi   94

Now Michelle and Ivanka Are Neighbors 97

Why Won't This Career Die? 104

Raising Baby Hitler 109

You May Already Be Running 116

The Privilege Tree 119

Part III

THIS FOLLOWS

Excuse Me, Director, I Have Some Questions
About My Role in the Spring Play as a Crisis Actor 125

Everything You Wanted to Know About Deep
State But Were Too Scared to Ask 128

Some Classic Episodes of Trump's Space Force 132

Welcome to AP U.S. History! Everyone Say Hi
to the Tank and the 150 Heavily Armed Men. 135

Part IV

MODEST PROPOSALS
AND OTHER COMMENTARY

A Good Time to Talk About Gun Laws 139

I Am Sick of These Children Demanding Safe Spaces 141

This Magic Is Too Strong to Stop 144

How to Sleep at Night When Families Are Being
Separated at the Border 146

Play the "Woman Card" and Reap These Rewards   *149*

That Five-Year-Old Refugee Has Diabolical Plans   *152*

I Will Not Take My Husband's Name   *155*

Part V

How Not to Do Things Wrong

Famous Quotes, the Way a Woman Ought to
Say Them in a Meeting   *159*

Some Interpersonal Verbs, Conjugated by Gender   *162*

How to Fact-Check   *166*

How to Speak Woman   *168*

How to Parent Wrong   *170*

What to Call Racist Remarks Instead of
Calling Them Racist Remarks   *175*

So, You Must Speak to the Woman Who Is
Wearing Headphones   *177*

Part VI

Finally, We Hear from Men, Measles, and a Pigeon

Please Stop Vaccinating Your Children. I Want
to Go to Disneyland.   *183*

Sorry, I Obey the Billy Graham Rule   *186*

I Am a State Legislator, and I Am Here to
Substitute-Teach Your Biology Class   *189*

Male Authors Describe Men in Literature Right   *193*

Surprise! I'm Back, and I Atoned   *198*

Without the Swimsuit Part of Miss America, When
Will I Be Able to Judge Women's Appearances?   *202*

I'm Fine with Women in Power, Just Not This
One Specific Woman Currently in Power   *205*

I Am in Favor of Confederate Statues. I Am
Definitely Not a Pigeon.   *208*

Coda   *213*

Acknowledgments   *215*

Introduction

RELAX. NOTHING IS WRONG.

There are cretins and goofs who will tell you that this is a bad time to be alive. Or, worse, an "interesting" time to be alive. They want to fill your head with lies—for instance, that outdated horrors are still occurring, and, in addition, new bad things are happening, and if it were not for the ability to order pizza on your phone without speaking to another human being, there would be no good arguments for the present at all. This is simply not true.

Actually, this is a *wonderful* time to be alive.

We live in an age when anything is possible. Those aforementioned cretins would phrase this another way: Things that once seemed unthinkable are now commonplace. Maybe that sounds bad to you. If it does, you are wrong. Also, you are a coward. Coward! I will explain to you all the wonderful things about being alive today very slowly and carefully so that even a child could comprehend them, keeping in mind that I despise children.

Things that humankind feared for millennia—certain sorts of bears, very big clouds, the weather more generally, large insects, snakes, the creatures who live in the oceans' plumbless depths—now fear us. We are putting the final nail in the tiny coffin of the poisonous frog; next we will tackle the ocelot. The dark, deep rainforests full of things that go hrrrr hrrrrr bump-kawwww shhshhshh cooooee in the night—they fall before us, acres a day, and their secrets vanish with them. Do not heed the scientists who say that these secrets could save us, could cure diseases. That is only the forest's vile whispering to save its own life, and soon we shall be rid of it for good.

For too many years, we bent the knee to the climate. We let it be hot in some places and cold in other places. We went around meekly putting up umbrellas and donning thick parkas and sleeping next to blocks of ice, because we (fools that we were) thought that we could do nothing to change it. We were forced to get out of the ocean and walk on the dry land and build cities on the dry land. Now see what we have done! Soon there will be water where there was land, and we will have gotten vengeance on the ice for the horrors it inflicted on our most titanic boat (the *Titanic*). The climate bows before us. We are not under the weather any longer. Now we soar above it in our magnificent jet airplanes, trailing carbon behind! The atmosphere will have carbon in it until we say otherwise, and the atmosphere will thank us.

Generations of parents once told their children not to be afraid to go to school—"What is the worst thing that could happen?" Now they see the possibilities. Now we all see them everywhere! Things we never thought could happen at places of worship, at concerts, at shopping malls, at movie theaters, at schools, at schools, at offices, at places of worship, at schools, in parking lots, at places of worship—they happen, and keep happening. Perhaps it once seemed unthinkable that people would fail to take action if such things did indeed occur—but that is the glory of the present time! People are doing the unthinkable every day!

And that is not the only good news! Things we feared lost decades ago are back and thriving. The Nazi, the Confederate, and the measle are all being tenderly reintroduced to their former habitats, where they seem to be flourishing, with a little periodic encouragement from above. Pollutants are being joyfully reunited with their ancestral rivers. Even the dread wide-leg pant is now frequently sighted in the wild.

And it is not only the reintroduction of these treasures to the landscape that has so gladdened our hearts and spread out such wide and tempting vistas before us. Also to the realm of government do these great gains extend.

Before, if someone had told you that they wanted to be put in charge of a large section of the government even though they knew nothing about it and perhaps wanted to co-opt it for personal profit, you would have told them to dream a different dream. You would have told them that this simply could not happen. People would not permit it. Well, you were wrong.

And that was not all. Before, for instance, there were certain things that we could not imagine a president would say. There were certain things, for instance, that we could not imagine a president would do. There were certain people, for instance, that we could not imagine would be placed in charge of anything, let alone the government of the United States of America. But no longer!

Indeed, we have much less need of imagination than we did before. Once people could make whole careers conjuring up outlandish things that were not happening. No longer! Now—we need simply watch. Caricaturists are out of business, joining the ranks of travel agents and most (but not all) of the people who scan and bag purchases at the drugstore. We have become our own parodies, eliminating waste and redundancy. This kind of efficiency is what has allowed us to thrive at home and drop jaws abroad. We have killed off satire once and for all. It is dead. Long live reality!

Which is to say, that it is a wonderful time to be alive. Yes, wonderful! How marvelous to be stepping out of the thick mists of confusing facts and up toward the light of perfect clarity. How glorious to live in an age when things that once were fairy tales are now seen, daily, to be completely real—children sticking their slim fingers through the bars of cages, emperors with no clothes, women with their voices ripped out. Galileo would probably love to be alive now. So would Jesus, who, I believe, is scheduled to arrive shortly.

Yes, now is the best time. Nothing is off limits. Perhaps it was a brief folly to think that anything was ever off limits. Perhaps the so-called unthinkable has always been commonplace and it was only that a few lucky people did not notice. Well, we know better now. No one has any idea what the next day will bring! Time itself seems to have taken on previously unimagined dimensions! The unthinkable is happening every day! We have emerged from the close darkness of Before, shedding old scientific precautions and pushing aside all the warnings of the past, to stand bravely, to gaze unblinkingly directly into the sun!

NOTHING IS WRONG
AND HERE IS WHY

Prologue

Welcome to the
New Physics!

YOU MAY EXPERIENCE some temporal discomfort.

It has been sixty years and you have barely crossed the span from Monday until Tuesday.

You entered the week comparatively young and spry and now you are a withered and wretched crone, demanding ointment, and things that you could swear happened yesterday were simultaneously three hundred years ago and never.

This is normal. This is how time works now.

Friday is both twice a week and not at all.

Each Friday lasts six years.

Tuesdays are only sometimes.

If you pause to look down at your phone in the middle of a routine activity, you will look up and see a barren, unfamiliar landscape and your hands will be covered in cobwebs. You are now three hundred years older than you were and you remember things no one else does and speak in a language that has been all but forgotten.

Do not panic. This is quite common.

Sometimes you will find yourself describing an event from the remote past and find that, in fact, it happened yesterday.

Sometimes you will find yourself describing an event from the recent past and find that, in fact, it happened never.

This mistake is common. Be sure to check your news with the news that has been Approved!

You may also notice that events happen and then unhappen. This, again, is normal. This is a sign that you are in this timeline with the rest of us.

Something may be very wise and smart and good to do and then it may never have occurred. Then all evidence of it may be buried. People may be very close to power and then they may vanish like ghosts. Things flicker in and out of existence. This is because only some of these things are being observed, although it is also possible that someone is meddling with the timeline and you should not mind it. Better, with these timelines, to leave well enough alone.

Q: Given all this confusion about time, should you be moisturizing?

A: Oh god, you should.

A: Moisturize, moisturize quickly. Absolutely you should moisturize. Oh, moisturize, without a doubt!

And do not panic. It does no one any good to panic.

You may think: Am I being sucked into a black hole? Is this not how time works when you are being sucked into a black hole?

The good news about approaching a black hole is that you will live a very long time.

The bad news about approaching a black hole is that you will never die.

The best news is that as you are sucked into this hole, you get to relive some critical moments of the recent past!

Relax and surrender to the new physics!

Part I

THE BRIGHTEST TIMELINE

YOU MAY FEEL THAT YOU UNDERSTAND WHAT has been happening for the past four years, but I assure you, you do not. Probably at some point you have imbibed a Bad Fact by mistake, instead of a True Fact. A Bad Fact makes you uneasy when you contemplate it. A Bad Fact has a seasick feeling about it. You may feel that things are going wrong, and that you are powerless to stop them. I pity you! It is time to expel such Bad Facts from your system! Embrace True Facts. Don't you want to see the world as it is, in all its shining glory and magnificence?! I want you to see it that way, as I see it. I am much happier now that I see things correctly. Are you not sick of seeing only failures and hobgoblins? Hold still, I am going to show you everything that is beautiful and true. Hold still, and listen.

Chris Christie's Wordless Screaming

It was March of 2016. Donald J. Trump was securing his party's nomination. And behind him stood Chris Christie, who made a face of such absolute horror that it filled the minds of all who beheld it with Bad Facts. A description of it follows, which you must certainly purge from your memory as quickly as you can.

Is Chris Christie okay?

I believe that Donald Trump was talking, tonight, and that he, in fact, held an entire press conference. But it was impossible to hear him over Chris Christie's eyes.

Chris Christie spent the entire speech screaming wordlessly. I have never seen someone scream so loudly without using his mouth before. It would have been remarkable if it had not been so terrifying.

Sometimes, at night, do you still hear them, Clarice? The screaming of the Christies?

His were the eyes of a man who has gazed into the abyss, and the abyss gazed back, and then he endorsed the abyss.

It was not a thousand-yard stare. That would understate the vast and impenetrable distance it encompassed.

He looked as if he had seen a ghost and the ghost had made him watch Mufasa die again.

He had the eyes of a man who has looked into the heart of light, the silence. A man who had seen the moment of his greatness flicker, and seen the eternal footman hold his coat, and snicker.

And, in short, he looked afraid.

He had the face of a man who has used his third wish and realized too late that "may my family never starve" could be twisted to mean that the genie should murder his entire family.

He had the face of a man who has just realized his own mortality.

Look into those eyes and try to deny that Chris Christie has seen something.

Someone just told Chris Christie that there is no God. Or Chris Christie has just discovered that God does exist but She is an enormous snake who hates or is indifferent to mankind. Or Chris Christie has just discovered that there is no God but that Hell is real.

"When are they coming to airlift me out?" Chris Christie's eyes are pleading. "Please tell me that they are coming and that it is soon." But then his expression hardens. Chris Christie knows that they are not coming back for him.

This is his life now.

Soon he must return to the plane onto which Trump humiliatingly sent him before. Soon he must return to the small cupboard under the stairs where he is kept and occasionally thrown small slivers of metaphorical raw meat. When he asked to be part of Trump's cabinet he never thought to specify "presidential cabinet, of course, not a literal cabinet underground where the ventilation is poor and there is no light." It just did not occur to him. Why would it?

And now it is too late.

Nobody is coming for you, Chris Christie. Nobody is coming to save you.

Chris Christie has seen things. Things you wouldn't believe. Things that would make your hair fall out and turn gray all at once. But he cannot speak of them. He can only stand there. Chris Christie is the bearer of a hideous knowledge that hangs on him like a horrible weight. But he has no way to say it.

He is embroidering this hideous truth very slowly onto a handkerchief, but it will not be ready in time.

Chris Christie must stand and watch as his city is overrun with Imperial troops and his friends are frozen in carbonite.

Chris Christie has the glazed and terrified look of someone who has traded his inheritance for no pottage at all, who has watched his credibility dry up and is about to be led back to his basement cage, having lost Winterfell for good.

Chris Christie is realizing that the steak he gets to eat inside the Matrix is not worth this.

Chris Christie has made a yuge mistake.

Donald Trump won at least seven states on Super Tuesday. His path to the nomination is clear.

Chris Christie has no mouth, but he must scream.

March 2, 2016

Waiting for Pivot:
A GOP Tragicomedy

THAT YEAR WAS A TIME when people thought Donald Trump might "pivot" to a "more presidential" tone. It was a time of much waiting.

Vladimir Ryan and Estragon Priebus, members of the GOP establishment, sit glumly in rags beneath a small leafless tree, next to a slowly decomposing elephant carcass. They wear matching flag pins. Estragon struggles mightily to remove his "Jeb 2016" button. At last it comes off with a pop.

ESTRAGON: Nothing to be done.

VLADIMIR: I'm beginning to come around to that opinion.

ESTRAGON: Let's go.

VLADIMIR: We can't.

ESTRAGON: Why not?

VLADIMIR: We're waiting for pivot.

ESTRAGON: For pivot?

VLADIMIR: The Trump pivot. To the general.

ESTRAGON: He pivots?

VLADIMIR: They say he pivots. He promised. He's going to be presidential.

ESTRAGON: Presidential Trump.

VLADIMIR: Exactly so.

ESTRAGON: I'll believe it when I see it.

VLADIMIR: We'll see it. (less confident) Just wait.

They wait. The sun sets. The moon rises. The elephant carcass does not stir. On TV, Donald Trump denounces Mexican judges and doubles down on his ban on Muslim immigrants.

ESTRAGON: Didi?

VLADIMIR: Yes, Gopgop?

ESTRAGON: How long?

VLADIMIR: What?

ESTRAGON: How long are we to wait here until he pivots?

VLADIMIR: He'll pivot. You'll see.

ESTRAGON: I'm frightened.

Vladimir fumbles in his pocket and finds a carrot.

VLADIMIR: Eat this.

ESTRAGON: What good will an old carrot do if I'm frightened?

VLADIMIR: (philosophical) It will accustom you to stomaching unpleasant old things that are orange in color.

Estragon begins to weep.

VLADIMIR: Gopgop, don't cry.

ESTRAGON: How can I help it? Have you read his quotes? Have you read his poll numbers?

VLADIMIR: No.

ESTRAGON: Will there be anything left of us?

Long silence. In the audience, a protester is beaten up and dragged away.

ESTRAGON: Do you think he's going to pivot soon?

VLADIMIR: I thought he would pivot after May.

ESTRAGON: May?

VLADIMIR: I thought he would pivot after Orlando.

Estragon: Orlando?

Vladimir: It was in the news.

Estragon looks at him blankly.

Vladimir: It was in the news. He responded to it by saying awful things.

Estragon: That sounds just like everything else.

He munches the carrot forlornly.

Estragon: I will try to remember.

Frustrated, he removes his flag pin, then puts it back on.

Estragon: No, I can't, I can't.

Vladimir: We mustn't lose hope.

Estragon: What day is it?

Vladimir: Super Tuesday. (He removes his pin and examines it.) But not super. Or even, perhaps, Tuesday.

Estragon: Have we always been here, waiting?

Vladimir: Surely not.

Estragon: How long have we been here?

Vladimir: Days.

Estragon: Weeks.

Vladimir: Months?

Estragon: Years?

Vladimir: You're sure it was here we were to wait?

Estragon: This is Cleveland, isn't it?

Vladimir: I don't know. Every place looks the same.

Estragon: Didn't we have a party, once?

Vladimir: I don't remember.

Estragon: Everything was red. There were balloons.

Vladimir: I can't remember.

Estragon: He said he'd pivot. He promised.

Vladimir: He didn't promise. Paul Manafort promised.

ESTRAGON: Who?

VLADIMIR: Paul Manafort comes every day and promises he'll pivot.

ESTRAGON: How do we know he can be presidential?

VLADIMIR: Eat your carrot.

ESTRAGON: What does Presidential Trump look like?

VLADIMIR: I don't know. I've never seen him.

ESTRAGON: (uncertainly) We would know him if we saw him.

VLADIMIR: Certainly we would.

ESTRAGON: What can we do in the meantime?

VLADIMIR: Speak generally.

ESTRAGON: Generally.

VLADIMIR: Speak of the nominee.

ESTRAGON: Hedge.

VLADIMIR: Obfuscate.

ESTRAGON: Find another one?

VLADIMIR: Another one? What other? There is no one else!

ESTRAGON: But all the same.

VLADIMIR: Who did we used to be? Do you remember? Didn't we used to have ideas?

ESTRAGON: I don't know.

VLADIMIR: Didn't we used to have values?

ESTRAGON: You fed me a carrot once. That's a value.

VLADIMIR: True.

ESTRAGON: Didi, I'm scared.

VLADIMIR: Shhh. It'll be all right.

ESTRAGON: Yesterday he beat me. He kicked me and took my phone. He grabbed it and tweeted, "Reports of discord are pure fiction. Rs will win in Nov!"

VLADIMIR: I wouldn't have let him.

ESTRAGON: You couldn't have stopped him.

VLADIMIR: I would have stopped you from doing whatever it was you did before he began to beat you.

ESTRAGON: Perhaps.

He unpins his flag pin and pins it on Vladimir. After some deliberation, Vladimir unpins his pin and pins it on Estragon. They pass the pins back and forth.

ESTRAGON: What do we do now?

VLADIMIR: We could start all over again, perhaps.

ESTRAGON: You can start from anything. From Romney.

VLADIMIR: Yes, but you have to have the delegates. Sleep.

ESTRAGON: I can't.

Vladimir goes over to Estragon and begins to sing soothingly.

VLADIMIR: Reagan Reagan Reagan Reagan Reagan Reagan

Enter Paul Manafort.

PAUL MANAFORT: Mister?

VLADIMIR: You have a message from Mr. Trump?

PAUL MANAFORT: Yes.

PAUL MANAFORT: Mr. Trump told me to tell you that he won't pivot today but surely tomorrow.

VLADIMIR: Is that all?

PAUL MANAFORT: Yes sir.

He makes to exit.

VLADIMIR: Paul?

PAUL MANAFORT: Yes sir.

VLADIMIR: What does it look like, this pivot to the general?

PAUL MANAFORT: Presidential.

VLADIMIR: Presidential how?

PAUL MANAFORT: So presidential that you will not believe it. So presidential you will be bored to tears.

VLADIMIR: God help us.

PAUL MANAFORT: What am I to tell Mr. Trump?

VLADIMIR: Tell him—tell him you saw me.

Paul Manafort makes to go.

VLADIMIR: Tell him you—you saw me. And it was a productive conversation. About values. Tell him you saw us and we're waiting here. Don't come back the same way tomorrow!

Paul Manafort exits. One of the bones of the elephant carcass twitches, then shatters.

Estragon suddenly sits bolt upright.

ESTRAGON: NO!

VLADIMIR: What's wrong with you?

ESTRAGON: Nothing. Let's go. Let's vote for Hillary. Let's run a third party. Let's denounce him. Let's do anything!

VLADIMIR: We can't.

ESTRAGON: Why not?

VLADIMIR: We're waiting.

ESTRAGON: What for?

VLADIMIR: The pivot.

ESTRAGON: He didn't pivot today?

VLADIMIR: No. He fired Corey Lewandowski. That's almost a pivot.

ESTRAGON: And now it's too late.

VLADIMIR: Yes, now it's night.

ESTRAGON: And if we dropped him? (pause) And if we dropped him?

VLADIMIR: He'd punish us.

ESTRAGON: Worse?

VLADIMIR: I don't know. (pause) Everything's dead.
    Even the elephant.

ESTRAGON: Yes.

VLADIMIR: We could end it all. That might be best.

ESTRAGON: Tomorrow.

VLADIMIR: Unless he pivots.

ESTRAGON: Then we'll be saved.

VLADIMIR: Perhaps not even then.

ESTRAGON: No.

He takes off his flag pin.

VLADIMIR: Well. Shall we go?

ESTRAGON: Yes. Let's go.

They do not move.

June 20, 2016

Nasty Women

Such a nasty woman.

—DONALD TRUMP, IN THE COURSE OF A
PRESIDENTIAL DEBATE, DESCRIBING
HILLARY CLINTON. HE COULD NOT HOPE
TO GUESS THE TRUTH OF HIS WORDS!

THE NASTY WOMEN GATHER on the heath just after midnight. It is Nasty Women's Sabbath, Election Eve, and they must make haste.

Their sturdy he-goats and their broomsticks are parked with the valet. Beyond the circle, their familiar owls and toads and pussycats strut back and forth, boasting of being grabbed or not grabbed.

A will-o'-the-wisp zigzags back and forth over the assemblage. (It is bad with directions, like a nasty woman.)

They have much to do and the hour is late.

They must sabotage the career of an upwardly mobile young general named Macbeth.

They must lure an old wizard into a cave and lock him there so that Camelot may fall.

They must finish Ron and Harry's homework for them (again).

They must turn some people into newts and let some of them get better and let others run for office and go on prime-time cable.

They must transform all of Odysseus's sailors into swine and then back again, get Sabrina through high school, freeze Narnia permanently, complete all sorts of housework for Samantha Stevens.

They have a good many apples to poison and drug and mermaid voices to steal and little dogs to get, too.

And then they have an election to rig.

They must make haste. The vagenda is quite full.

They gather around the bubbling cauldron as the squirrels scurry off into hiding and the bats fly in.

One particularly nasty woman who has been juggling a lot at home and at work flies in late on her Swiffer and apologizes; she has not even had time to put a wart on her nose or a bat into her hair. Nasty women know that it only looks easy.

The nasty women gather around the cauldron and lean in.

They lean in with the ingredients that they have been gathering for days, for years, to make the potion potent.

Eye of newt. Wool of bat. Woman cards, both tarot and credit. Binders. Lemons. Lemonade. Letters to the editor saying that a woman could not govern at that time of month. (In fact she would be at the height of her power and capable of unleashing the maximum number of moon-sicknesses against our enemies, but the nasty women do not stoop to correct this.)

They toss in pieces of meat and legs with nothing else attached and dolls and sweethearts and sugars and all the other things they were told to be, and like it.

They drop in paradoxes: powerful rings that give you everything and keep you from getting the job, heels that only move forward by moving backward, skirts that are too long and too short at the same time, comic book drawings whose anatomy defies gravity, suits that become pantsuits when a woman slips them on, enchanted shirts and skirts and sweaters that can ask for it, whatever it is, on their own. They take the essence of a million locker rooms wrung out of towels and drop it in, one drip at a time. Then stir.

They sprinkle it with the brains of the people who did not recognize that they were doctors, pepper it with ground-up essays by respected men asking why women aren't funny, whip in six pounds of pressure and demands for perfection. They drizzle it with the laughter of women in commercials holding salads and the rueful smiles of women in commercials peddling digestive yogurts. They toss in some armpit hair and a wizened old bat, just to be safe. And wine. Plenty of wine. And cold bathwater. Then they leave it to simmer.

And they whisper incantations into it, too. They whisper to it years of shame and blame and what-were-you-wearing and boys-will-be-boys. They tell the formless mass in the cauldron tales of the too many times that they were told they were too much. Too loud. Too emotional. Too bossy. Too . . . insufficiently smiling. They whisper the words shouted at them as they walked down the streets. The words typed at them when their minds traveled through the Internet. They repeat every concession they were told to make so that they took up less space. Every time they were too mean or too nice or shaped wrong. Every time they were told they were different, other, objects, the princess at the end of the quest, the grab-bag prize for the end of the party.

They pour them all into a terrible and bitter brew and stir to taste.

It tastes nasty. It is the taste of why we cannot have nice things, and they are used to that.

Perhaps if the potion works, they will not have to be.

The nasty women have a great deal to do before the moon sinks back beneath the horizon.

But that is all right. They know how to get things done.

October 20, 2016

Donald Trump and His Sons Will Never Talk Business Again

Donald Trump has been blessed with two tall and healthy adult sons who have slain numerous wild beasts using only sticks that spit fire. They are married to human women, and their hair is sleek and glossy like the back of a marmot. They possess the right number of teeth. Donald Trump loves to speak to them and give them his counsel, and the one great tragedy of his presidency was that he was very strictly told he could no longer talk business with them. How could he? They were to manage the Trump Organization in trust, and he had vowed not to know anything about its deals and doings until he read about it in the newspaper—or, to be realistic, saw it on TV. Taking him at his word, here is a look at that first year without talk of business.

WINTER:

Donald Trump, Eric, and Don Jr. sit around the dinner table. "So," Trump says. "How are things?"

Eric glances nervously at his brother. "Things?"

"Not business things, obviously," Trump corrects, glancing down the table at the ethics adviser who has been following them around since this began. "You things."

"Good," Eric says. "They're good."

A long silence ensues.

"Just good?" Trump asks.

"Great," Eric corrects. His lower lip quivers. "Always great, Pop."

"That's good," Trump says. "I like to hear that."

SPRING:

"What did you do today?" Trump asks.

"Well, Pop, I did a lot of things," Eric says.

"You know we can't talk about them," Don Jr. says.

"I ate a healthy breakfast," Eric adds, quickly. "Fruit."

"Huh," Donald says. "Fruit."

Don Jr.'s fork clicks on his plate. "I had a waffle."

"Good for you, Don," Trump says. "I like waffles."

"I'm just trying to watch my health," Eric says, a little defensively.

"Well," Donald says, "that's important, too."

Silence falls again. Don Jr.'s fork clinks.

SUMMER:

"So things are good?" Donald asks.

"Yes," Eric says.

"Good." Donald eats a mouthful of mashed potatoes. "You do anything else? Read a book?"

Don shakes his head.

"No," Trump says. "I didn't figure you would have. Probably don't have time, what with all the—"

Eric touches his arm and shakes his head gently.

Autumn:

"I can't believe they won't let me talk to my sons!" Trump says. "Unbelievable!"

The ethics adviser shakes his head. "No," he says. "You can talk to them as much as you want. Just not about business."

"What else is there to talk about?"

"Well," the adviser suggests, "your feelings—or—your thoughts, or memories you had together, or—things like that."

A long silence ensues.

"I never felt my father loved me," Donald Trump says, suddenly. "I never felt my father knew me. He seemed to see me as an extension of himself that he could mold and do with as he pleased. I never felt he saw me there at all."

"But, Pop," Eric says. His voice cracks.

"I'm almost afraid to ask whether the two of you felt the same way."

"I didn't," Don Jr. says.

"A memory—" Trump says. "I remember when I held you for the first time, at the hospital, before I gave you back to the people who changed you and fed you and cleaned you and loved you until you were old enough to talk to like a reasonable man—and I always wished I'd held on longer. When I saw you again, you were a little stranger in a little suit." Trump sighs. "But it's no good, regretting things. It makes you soft."

"I never thought you were soft, Pop," Eric says.

"I wish I'd changed your diapers," Donald Trump says. "Even once. Is that too weird to say?"

"Yes," Don Jr. says.

"Pop," Eric asks earnestly, "what do you do when you get lonely?

"Good potatoes," Don Jr. says. "Really good."

"Sometimes I wonder if I will be saved," Trump says. "I have such dreams—I could not begin to tell you. I wake up and I cry out for my mother and then for your mother and then I remember that the woman who would answer is a stranger, and I have nothing to say to her. What can I say to her?"

Eric nervously reaches out to touch his shoulder. They sit there a moment.

"There are so many things about myself—so many things!—and in me they look strong, and good, but when I see them in you, my heart breaks a little."

"Pop—" Eric says. His voice cracks. "Do you love me?"

"Of course," Trump says. "Do you doubt it?"

"Never once, ever in my life, have I felt truly secure that I was loved," Eric says. "Not since you sent my nanny back to London."

"I didn't know we'd sent her," Donald says.

"I know," Eric says. "That was what hurt the most."

"I'm sorry. Group hug?" Trump asks.

He glances down the table at the ethics adviser.

"Pop, I wrote a poem this week."

"A poem?"

"Do you have the poem with you, son?" Trump asks. "Let's hear it."

Eric reaches into his pocket and pulls out a folded sheet of lined paper with "Daddy" written on the top in uneven large block letters.

Don Jr. hits his head against the table. "Dad," he says, "Dad, *please,* you have to divest."

"What?" Trump looks wildly at him.

"If you divest, you can end this, and we'll never have to do this, ever again."

"Oh," Trump says. "Thank God."

Eric slowly folds the poem and puts it back into his pocket.

———————————

January 12, 2017

The True, Correct Story of What Happened at Donald Trump's Inauguration

Finally, Approved News! Here is the fair and unbiased story about the inauguration written in compliance with the Trump style guidelines that we should have been obeying all along.

NOTHING THAT HAS EVER HAPPENED or will ever happen was as great as Donald Trump's inauguration.

The crowd was magnificent and huge, bigger than any crowd had ever been before! It stretched all the way to the moon. The Pope, who was there, confirmed it.

"Thanks for being here, Pope," Donald Trump told him.

"Are you kidding? You're my best friend," the Pope said. "I wouldn't miss your big day for *anything*!" He gave Donald Trump a big high-five.

Everyone in the world had come there at great expense. They sold all their possessions—their homes, their *Hamilton* tickets, which were worthless to them—to raise money to come and see this great sight. They could not believe that a perfect being such as Donald Trump even existed. They thought that he was a myth or a legend or a decades-long series of fabrications.

But then they saw him, and their doubts fell away.

The media was there, too, and they were very sorry. "Donald," the newscasters said, "we were mean to you. We used to laugh and call you names. We were *no better* than all of the other reindeer. How can you ever forgive us?"

"Forgive you?" Donald Trump asked. "I've already forgotten." He smiled a big, beautiful smile. That was just who Donald Trump was: forgiving, like Jesus, but blond.

It was a wonderful start to the day.

Everyone liked Donald Trump's speech and the words that he used. They liked even more the part where he rolled up his sleeve and showed off his bicep. It was a great bicep. It made the Rock so upset to see it that he threw something down on the ground and said "darn."

Donald Trump pulled out a violin and played a solo, and then he pulled out a guitar and played an even sicker solo. The whole ground was soon covered with women's undergarments. (Millions of women were there to support Donald Trump, and they were all AT LEAST sevens.) Also, every woman that Donald Trump had ever dated was there, and they were not upset with him, just ashamed that they had not lived up to his required standard.

"Trump! Trump! Trump!" the crowd cheered.

Donald Trump touched many people in the crowd in a way that they all thought was welcome and appropriate, and he cured their ailments, from cancer to autism.

"If only we could bottle your touch," someone said, "children could stop getting vaccinated altogether."

Donald Trump winked. "Don't worry!" he said. "I'm on it!"

Then Donald Trump served loaves and fishes to everyone there. There were enough loaves and fishes for everyone, and they all were Made in America and said "TRUMP" on them. It was like the Oscars, but also like Woodstock, but also like the Super Bowl, but also like the Sermon on the Mount. If you were not there, you should just go home and die, because nothing in your life will have purpose or meaning by comparison, not even holding your newborn child in your arms or having health insurance. This specific experience is what FOMO was always worried about.

Bono, and Bruce Springsteen, and Elton John, and the Rolling Stones, and Beyoncé, and all the top artists were there. They fought hard over who would be allowed to sing. Finally Bruce Springsteen won. Bono cried and cried, and the other artists had to console him. When Bruce Springsteen had finished singing, he walked over to Donald Trump, extended his hand, and said, "You are the only real hero left in the world."

The people were so excited that they built a very special stone pyramid just for Donald Trump so that he would not have to wait until he died to see what his monument would look like. But they were silly to be concerned. Donald Trump will never die!

A little child was in the audience, and he started to cry because the emperor was wearing so many clothes. Also, he could tell that he was not and never had been racist.

Donald Trump's beautiful big family was there. His favorite childhood dog was there, too, back from the farm where he still lives to this day.

Donald Trump can talk to the animals, and his eyes are lasers. When the floor is lava, Donald Trump can walk on it, but only Donald Trump. When Donald Trump points his finger at you,

you have to lie down. But when other people point their fingers at Donald Trump, he does not have to. Donald Trump's block tower is the biggest. He does not need a nap or a snack. He has the longest, biggest attention span. Everyone loves Donald Trump, and what he has to say interests them.

Donald Trump is the star. People love him.

He won the popular vote, too.

January 24, 2017

Trump's Budget Makes Perfect Sense and Will Fix America, and I Will Tell You Why

From govinfo.gov:
Issued by the Office of Management and Budget
(OMB), the Budget of the United States Government
is a collection of documents that contains the budget
message of the President:

Title: **A New Foundation for American Greatness**

SOME PEOPLE ARE COMPLAINING THAT the budget proffered by the Trump administration, despite its wonderful macho-sounding name, is too vague and makes all sorts of cuts to needed programs in favor of increasing military spending by leaps and bounds. These people are wimps. Office of Management and Budget Director Mick Mulvaney has called it a "hard power budget," which is, I think, the name of an exercise program where you eat only what you can catch, pump up your guns, and then punch the impoverished in the face. This, conveniently, is also what the budget does.

This budget will make America a lean, mean fighting machine

with bulging, rippling muscles and not an ounce of fat. America has been weak and soft for too long. BUT HOW WILL I SURVIVE ON THIS BUDGET? you may be wondering. I AM A HUMAN CHILD, NOT A COSTLY FIGHTER JET. *You* may not survive, but that is because you are SOFT and WEAK, something this budget is designed to eliminate.

What are we cutting?

The State Department, by 29 percent: Right now, all the State Department's many qualified employees do is sit around being sad that they are never consulted about anything. This is, frankly, depressing, and it is best to put them out of their misery. Besides, they are only trained in Soft Diplomacy, like a woman would do, and NOBODY wants that. Only HARD POWER. With the money we will save on these sad public servants, we will be able to buy lots of GUNS and F-35s and other cool things that go BOOM and POW and PEW PEW PEW.

Environmental Protection Agency: We absolutely do not need this. Clean rivers and breathable air are making us SOFT and letting the Chinese and the Russians get the jump on us. We must go back to the America that was great, when the air was full of coal and danger and the way you could tell if the air was breathable was by carrying a canary around with you at all times, perched on your leathery, coal-dust-covered finger. Furthermore, we will cut funding to Superfund cleanup in the EPA because the only thing manlier than clean water is DIRTY water.

Agriculture Department: NO MORE OF THIS NAMBY-PAMBY "GATHERING" NONSENSE. We will be HUNTERS again. This is also why we are cutting the Special

Supplemental Nutrition Program for Women, Infants, and Children: Let them FIGHT for their meat or have NONE.

Commerce Department: This will lose its funding to prepare people for coastal disasters, because in the future we will all be so strong that we can stare down the sea and make it recede by flexing our bulging muscles.

Labor Department: There will be no LABOR in the future. Labor is what women do, I think. All fetuses will burst out of wombs brandishing an Uzi on each arm. (Also, we will cut the funding to the people who would have explained that this is not how birth or labor works.)

National Institutes of Health: We are decreasing funding because in the future we will cure disease by punching it, or, if that fails, sending drones after it. Also, we will buy more planes and guns to shoot airborne viruses out of the sky.

Affordable housing is a luxury and we are going to get rid of it. Donald Trump does not live in affordable housing and neither should you.

Historic sites: We don't need to fund them. Those parks have sassed the administration enough, and they must get what is coming to them.

A few other things we are cutting:

+ **Chemical Safety Board:** Give us CHEMICAL DANGER, which sounds way more metal.
+ **Corporation for Public Broadcasting:** Instead,

anyone who turns on the radio will be able to hear audio footage of a Trump son shooting a rare land mammal.

+ **National Endowment for the Arts:** The NEA will be destroyed and replaced with an armored helicopter with a shark painted on it.

+ **National Endowment for the Humanities:** The NEH will be replaced with half a fighter jet and a bunch of drones. This is the only art America needs.

+ **U.S. Institute of Peace:** Wimpy.

+ **U.S. Interagency Council on Homelessness:** We will all live outdoors in the new Hard Power America, and we will pump steel together and shout "GRRR," and there will be no mental illness because it is only in your mind.

+ **Woodrow Wilson International Center for Scholars:** This is counterintuitive given Wilson's track record of racism, which is no longer the handicap that it once was, but you must remember that he also tried to start the League of Nations, which was like the United Nations but more so.

There is a $2.6 billion line in the budget to pay for the wall until Mexico pays for the wall. I think? Sounds right. The education budget is also cut so I can't tell if this logic makes sense.

All schoolchildren will be taught by an F-35 wearing a Make America Great Again hat. They will also have new school choice options including the choice not to afford any school at all, because at school you are taught things like grammar and pronouns and spelling and history, and these are all potentially inimical to the future we are trying to build. We will also be cutting Meals on Wheels, as well as after-school programs to feed children, because they are not improving performance as we would like. Feed children just to feed them? What are we, SOFT? No. No we are not.

AMERICA WILL BE STRONGER THAN IT HAS EVER BEEN! Anyone who survives will be a gun covered in the fur of a rare mammal, capable of fighting disease with a single muscular flex. RAW POWER! HARD RAW POWER GRRRRRR HISSS POW!

It will be great.

*Author's Note: This story was so accurate and true that the Trump White House sent it out in its 1600 Daily email of Good, True, Accurate News! This goes to show that we can all be Real News if we set our minds to it.**

March 16, 2017

---

* This is 100 percent not a parody. They actually did this. This is one of exactly thirty-five sincere sentences in this book! Write your best guesses about the others on a postcard and send them to Mike Pence, One Observatory Drive, and he will tell you if you were right!

Every Story I Have Read About Trump Supporters in the Past Week

Many so-called Journalists have gone to so-called Real so-called America in order to describe the thoughts and sentiments of Trump supporters as his agenda progresses across the land, ravaging everything in its path. It is important that we hear this story again and again, as many times as possible! I will tell it to you now, but better.

IN THE SHADOW of the old flag factory, Craig Slabornik sits whittling away on a rusty nail, his only hobby since the plant shut down. He is an American like millions of Americans, and he has no regrets about pulling the lever for Donald Trump in November—twice, in fact, which Craig says is just more evidence of the voter fraud plaguing the country. Craig is a contradiction, but he does not know it.

Each morning he arrives at the Blue Plate Diner and tries to make sense of it all. The regulars are already there. Lydia Borkle lives in an old shoe in the tiny town of Tempe Work Only, Arizona, where the factory has just rusted away into a pile of gears and dust. The jobs were replaced by robots, not shipped overseas, but try telling Lydia that. (I did, very slowly and patiently,

I thought, but she still became quite brusque.) Her one lifeline was an Obama-era jobs training program, but she says that she does not regret her vote for Trump and likes what he says about business. She makes a point of telling me that she is not racist, but I think she probably is, a little.

Next to her sits Linda Blarnik. Like the rusty hubcaps hanging on the wall behind her, she was made in America fifty years ago, back when this town made things, a time she still remembers fondly. She says she has had just enough of the "coastal elitist media who keep showing up to write mean things about my town and my life, like that thing just now where you said I was like a hubcap, yes you, stop writing I can see over your shoulder." Mournfully a whistle blows behind her, the whistle of a train that does not stop in this America any longer.

Linda's sister, Carla Blarnik, is married to an undocumented immigrant yet voted for Trump, who has vowed an increase in deportations. Asked to explain this contradiction, she shrugs. "Do not tell Bert this," she says, "but I have been trying to find an unobtrusive way to break up the marriage for years and this seemed like just the loophole I was waiting for." Huh. Okay.

Their waiter is David Mattress, a sentient robot who will be shut down if Trump's budget is put into practice. He loves Trump, insofar as love is possible for him. When asked, "Don't you realize the contradiction of this position?" the other regulars leap up and shout at me because the last time this question was posed to him, David short-circuited and emitted large quantities of smoke. "First that magazine writer," Linda scolds me, gesturing to a table in the corner where six other journalists sit writing versions of this same article, "now *you*."

Mark Hooglats lives inside Obamacare, don't ask him how. He voted for Trump. He will vote for Trump again, maybe up to ten times if he does the thing with the economy. He is excited that Trump has said "God" out loud for what he believes is the first time in the past eight years. (It *isn't*.)

In the corner, under a picture of George Washington that is cracked and broken and stained with tobacco juice, lies Herm Slabornik. Herm is encased in a cryogenic tube that will be unplugged if Trump gets his way. According to a note on his cryotube, he knows what Trump said about unplugging tubes but he does not think Trump would unplug him personally. He will vote for Trump again in 2020, provided he is not unplugged. Also, he hates Obamacare.

Glom Pfeffernitz lives in a rusty kettle. Trump's plan will definitely repossess his kettle, but he does not believe me when I tell him this. "I just don't think he'd do that," Glom repeats. Glom's priority is filling the lakes with waste because he remembers when he was a kid and the lakes used to glow, and he wants to get back to those great days. He says his number one priority is keeping telephones away from the undeserving poor.

Claudia Barknappen, the owner of the diner, wipes her hands on her faded God Bless America apron. She is taken aback to see that Trump's budget would replace her home with a sinkhole, but she says that she is reserving judgment and likes how much he hates immigrants. "We've got to give him a chance," she observes. She says that one time Trump showed up at her home and hit her dog with a broom, but in her mind this amounts to no more than one strike. She knows that she can change Trump with love, not that he needs to change at all. Behind her, an eagle falls out of a tree and dies.

April 4, 2017

This Is Not a Crisis,
Republicans Say,
as a Large Spider
Slowly Devours Them

I WOULD RECOGNIZE A CRISIS if it were happening.

When the president seized me, stunned me with his venom, and covered me with digestive fluid from his chelicerae, I was initially taken aback, but I reassured myself with this thought: President Richard Nixon never did that.

I know history.

This is clearly not the end of the world. That would be more clearly labeled and would be brought about by the other party. And the weather would be more ominous. Ravens would squawk, and the sky would turn red. It would not occur on a Tuesday when I had made other plans.

Okay, the firing of FBI Director James Comey looked bad. And when the president stunned him, pierced him with his fangs, wrapped him in a thick cocoon of impenetrable webbing, and left him to hang there for days, that timing was also poor. It doesn't seem as though it was what the FBI wanted or what the deputy attorney general wanted, either. But the American people voted for change! And the president is not Nixon. Nixon fired people on a Saturday, whereas this happened on a Tuesday.

He does not sweat and look pale on TV, which Nixon always

did. Also, history plainly states that Nixon was born in 1913, one of several siblings, whereas the president was born in 1946, one of 3,000 eggs. Already we are seeing huge discrepancies! Nixon had only two legs.

Nixon was married to a woman named Pat who wore Republican cloth coats. I think we can agree that we are talking about someone different. Come back when our leader has adopted a small dog named Checkers, and then we will see where we stand.

This has none of the historical signs of a crisis. We still believe in small government, and that doesn't have to change because the person or entity presiding over it happens to be a giant spider.

I think of the many norms that are still going strong as the digestive acid begins to eat its way through my flag pin.

We got an appointee for the Supreme Court! That, already, is a great accomplishment.

If this were a real crisis, there would be no other news. An alert would go over the TV. It would say, "Democracy Alert!" and make an unpleasant sound. In the meantime, I'm glad those Unicorn Frappuccinos are gone.

But the background music has not crescendoed. I look out the window, and the sun is shining. On the television the colorful heads are speaking as they have always spoken, and they are still not in agreement. I think. It is getting harder to see in here, and I feel a curious warmth spreading through all my appendages. I would not feel this way if something really serious were going on. The polls would reflect it, too.

I am still getting what I wanted. It is good to have someone in the Oval Office who shares my values: covering everything with giant webs, eating flies, and restoring our relationship with Russia. I think I once had other values but, well, winning is winning.

Also, we have yet to see what this will become.

It is quite possible that the thing spewing its webbing everywhere in the Oval Office is not in its final form. Perhaps it will ultimately look like Merrick Garland. We should wait. Really, everything depends on the next move. Which will, of course, set the terms for the move after that. All of which we must contemplate and look into.

It's very dark.

If we are ever in a point of real crisis, I will be the hero the country requires. I know that about myself. But in the meantime, I stand behind the president, who I am positive is not literally Nixon.

Besides, if it were really bad, Paul Ryan would say something.

I want to sleep.

If this were a crisis, something would be done by someone. A hero would emerge.

If there were an occasion, I would be rising to it. But I am not rising.

May 12, 2017

What the Ethics Chief Really Wanted to Say in His Resignation Letter

The Office of Government Ethics director, Walter Shaub, has submitted a letter of resignation. He will depart on July 19 to work for the nonpartisan Campaign Legal Center.

"The great privilege and honor of my career has been to lead OGE's staff and the community of ethics officials in the federal executive branch," he wrote. "They are committed to protecting the principle that public service is a public trust, requiring employees to place loyalty to the Constitution, the laws, and ethical principles above private gain."

Shaub told NPR that "the current situation has made it clear that the ethics program needs to be stronger than it is."

This was much less strongly worded than the previous draft, which ran as follows:

LISTEN, I HAVE TO RESIGN for my own mental health, because I am honestly starting to wonder if I am invisible.

Now that I am leaving, let me ask: Have you gotten any of the warnings about disclosures and conflicts of interest that I have sent for the past numerous months? It seems like you have, and it certainly looked like they had gone through, but—nothing. I go into rooms and clear my throat pointedly and no one even looks up from signing a directive to make sure that our desire to protect our drinking water does not interfere with making golf courses great again.

Most days I feel like I am dropping a copy of the emoluments clause into a dark deep black hole from which nothing, not even radiation, can escape.

Sometimes I send an email with very pointed italics saying "this doesn't seem okay" but—not even crickets. I think the crickets are dead. I go home and I am sometimes startled when people respond to my voice. Sometimes cats look right through me.

Ideally, we are supposed to suggest ways of resolving conflicts, but people have to WANT to resolve conflicts. Right now, the only blind trust that Donald Trump has is the blind trust that the American people have placed in him to run his business appropriately.

And what's worse is that, somehow, it seems like literally everyone outside the administration has gotten the idea that they ought to call me to tell me about ethics violations. I appreciate it. It makes me feel wanted, I guess. It is nice to have thousands upon thousands of calls. I think they think that I can stop it, somehow. But I can't. All I can do is suggest until I am blue in the face. And I am. If my face is still visible, which I sincerely doubt.

I hope that, in future, people understand what the Office of Government Ethics can and cannot do. What it can do is SUGGEST, even going so far as to use ITALICS, but we don't have investigative powers, and for a while I was worried we might not even be able to compel disclosures. That is up to Congress. I am not saying "please stop calling us," but I feel like people keep telling me about cats in trees under the misapprehension that I can run off and change into a lifesaving spandex outfit and rescue them, and in fact I am just a mild-mannered fellow who can write a memo saying that the cat ought to be looked into.

This is wearing on me, as it wears on the other employees. It seems wasteful to have an entire office of seventy people whose entire job is to make suggestions that nobody listens to. It makes us feel like ghosts.

After a certain point you could just get a printed sign that says DON'T DO ANY OF THIS and it might do as good a job, and the sign wouldn't get depressed and think to itself, "Is my whole life a waste? Does my voice even make a sound?"

Honestly, do we need an Office of Government Ethics? If this is how you're going to treat it, I think not. Sometimes I lie awake in the vast loneliness where I exist and no one takes notice of me, and I wonder if ethics might not be obsolete, anyway. They are cumbersome. They take sacrifices. They require you to comply and eliminate conflicts, not rush to conflicts and fan them. Never let it be said that Donald Trump backed down from a conflict. His business holdings reflect this, I think. I don't know. Nobody knows, because his tax returns are still a riddle wrapped in an enigma surrounded by an impenetrable wall of darkness and lawyers.

Speaking of lawyers, I understand that we are draining the swamp by filling the swamp with apex predators and letting them fight it out, so perhaps all these outdated rules about hiring lobbyists and industry types need to be chucked into the swamp too, to see if they survive. They probably won't, but that will mean less paperwork for everyone.

And I have had enough.

One thing remains for me to do, and then my journey is

ended. I will put ethics on my shoulder and walk and walk until I come to a place where no man knows what they are. Oops, I am already there. Well, never mind. I will continue to walk, because this is no way to live.

July 7, 2017

A Moderate Speaks: By God, Won't Someone Else Take a Stand?

THIS IS NOT THE SENATE that I believe in.

I look around and see only the ruin of this once-great democratic institution. What has become of the process? Where are the committees? Where is the deliberation?

This bill is bad, and it was made in a process that was even worse. The courageous thing to do would be to stand against it. And yet no one will, not even me.

I am disgusted.

Bills ought to be passed with deliberation by committees. Change should be achieved in a bipartisan manner. Incrementally, day by day, we should reach a consensus—not perfect, by any means, but something that we can be proud of, nonetheless. That is why, when this dangerous and secret bill came up for a vote, I said "Aye," in such a cold and cutting tone.

This place should not be vulnerable to the shifting winds of public opinion, like some sort of novelty windsock. The Senate was supposed to be like a saucer where the Founders could pour their coffee to cool it. Well, I don't think this saucer would cool any coffee, because this saucer is BROKEN. And now this nation is covered in coffee. By God! (This was more stirring in my head.)

We are supposed to make compromises. We are supposed to listen. But these sad days, no one will. Not even me.

This is no way to proceed. Is anyone in favor of this legislation? Do we even know what this is? It is happening so fast that I cannot be sure, but it seems to benefit no one except taxpayers in high-income brackets and those who delight in human suffering. We are doing the legislative equivalent of throwing darts at a wall, but the wall is made of human faces.

I have no idea what is passing and what is being debated. Everything around me is chaos. Out of the wreckage of the parliamentary procedure rides Mitch McConnell on a pale horse sowing destruction in his wake. I think we just agreed to push all wheelchairs, occupied or not, over a cliff somewhere, but honestly I have no idea.

Will you just stand by and let this happen? You must not, because I will.

Where are the courageous three or four people who are willing to stand alone with me against this? I can't do it without the cover of a courageous three or four people, and those people are nowhere to be found.

By God, what has become of the Senate? What has become of the nation's greatest deliberative body? It is time that someone else took a stand. This legislation we are throwing frantically up for a vote is a disgrace to the country, it is cruel, and we arrived at it the wrong way, and so I will not vote for it more than once.

After all, I am here to serve my constituents by doing what I think, after deliberation, is in their best interests. I am here because I believe people working together across the aisle to tackle the challenges facing America can pass laws that make people's lives better and easier. That is why I am here, in theory.

And I will gladly stand alone against this shameful process that threatens all that I hold dear by issuing a series of scathing statements to reporters on my way to vote for whatever this mystery bill is.

We are the equal of the executive, but we don't act like it. Well, we should start acting like it! Where is the brave man or woman who will go first? I eagerly await such a person.

This bill was not given the process it deserves. We should have deliberated in committee. We should have held hearings. We should have done this the right way. So I, for one, will fight it tooth and nail. I will do everything except vote against it.

Who will stand without me?

July 27, 2017

How Paul Manafort Came by $934,350 in Antique Carpets

Buried among the revelations in the indictment against former Trump campaign manager Paul Manafort—charging him with conspiracy to launder money, making false statements to the FBI, and more—is the fact that he paid $934,350 to an antique rug store in Alexandria. Everything else about this story is also amazing, but I do not want to lose sight of this: $934,350, over a period of years, for carpets!

Is not the simplest explanation the best and most likely to be true?

Maybe Paul Manafort just loves carpets, and he was not deluding anyone in any way. $934,350 is a totally reasonable amount of money to spend at a rug store. You can easily see how this would happen.

FIRST, YOU WALK INTO THE STORE, thinking you need a small and simple rug to bring the room together. You have lots of cash, for some reason. You can spend some on a rug, surely. Or what was the point of all your work abroad?

You look at some carpets. They all seem about the same, so you pick one at random.

"That one," you say.

The salesman nods sagely. "I see that you are someone with an eye for carpets," he says.

You have never thought of yourself as someone with an eye for carpets, but you always hate to disillusion people who have positive opinions of you, even when those people are salesmen. "Well," you say, modestly, spreading your hands. "I dabble. I like a good . . ." Frantically, you try to remember the attributes that a good carpet is supposed to have. "Piling."

"Ah yes," the salesman says, smoothly, "a good, tall pile. Then you had better come with me."

"I'm taking that one, of course," you add, gesturing at the first rug.

"Very good. That is, of course, $15,750," the salesman says. Without waiting for your response, he leads you into the next room. These carpets are, frankly, more than you are looking for, but you don't want to admit it. You point at a small one in the corner. "Seems good," you say.

"Ah," the salesman says, adding it to the stack, "you are more than a match for me! We must go to the special collection! Nothing less will do for a man like you."

"Er," you say. "I suppose we had better."

He throws open the door to another room, covered wall-to-wall with carpets. You drop your wallet in your nervousness and it entirely disappears into the deep, lush pile of one of them. The salesman has to send a wallet-sniffing dog in to retrieve it, and this costs an additional $7,400. You close your eyes and point at random to two carpets that you hope are not too expensive, but it turns out that they are $46,200. You call Cyprus to wire the money.

The salesman watches you intently. "I can see you are not finished with us yet," he says. "A true connoisseur! Your knowledge is magisterial! Do you wish to meet the Maestro?"

"Yes," you say, wilting a little inside.

The Maestro is a man in a fancy hat who is perched on a rolled-up carpet. When you come in, he gazes at you solemnly. "You are a man who knows what he wants," he says.

"That's me," you say.

"That is what she tells me." He gestures to the carpet next to him. "She sensed your presence," he says. "She will go home with you, she tells me."

"She," you say. You swallow. "That is, the carpet?"

The other salesman has appeared at your elbow with a glass of pricey champagne. "We will drink this to toast her new home," he says.

"Er," you say, feebly, "actually, I think I'm about carpeted out. Got what I came for, as it were."

"Mais non!" the salesman says. He is speaking French now, which makes everything sound twice as expensive as before. "Jamais!"

He unlocks a further door and leads you into an even more opulent room. It is full of carpets so beautiful you want to weep. They smell like home. The one in the middle is the finest yet. Looking on it, you know joy for the first time. A tag informs you that it was made lovingly by hand with entirely pure motives by the only good human being who remains in the world. It shows. "Climb on," the salesman says. "Together, you will fly."

You climb onto the carpet, feeling rather foolish.

"Look!" the salesmen cry, in raptures. "You are flying!"

You don't think you are flying, but the salesmen seem so impressed that you do not have the heart to disabuse them of this notion either. You mime flying around for a little bit and in the course of it you knock over an expensive lamp, lighting three carpets immediately on fire.

"I will add them to your bill," the first salesman says.

"Yes," you say. "I guess you'd better." You are blind with panic. All you want now is to get out of this store before you cost yourself any more money. In your haste to get up you knock over two more lamps. The whole room is on fire.

"That will be $934,350," the salesperson says.

"Ah," you say. "I will wire the money to you slowly over a period of years, how does that sound?"

"Fine," the salesman says. "Do you want over half a million dollars' worth of bespoke suits?"

You shrug. "I might as well, at this point," you say.

And that is probably how Paul Manafort wound up with those expenses that we now see listed. This is a perfectly logical explanation that involves no money laundering at all.

October 31, 2017

Melania Trump Wants to Spend Christmas on a Deserted Island (With Her Family)

> Q: *My name is Andy . . . I am 10 . . . If you could spend the holidays anywhere in the world, where would you go?*
> FLOTUS: *I would spend my holidays on a deserted island, a tropical island, with my family.*
>
> —WHITE HOUSE POOL REPORT, 12/7/2017

IT LOOKS NOTHING LIKE CHRISTMAS on the island.

It is full of nothing—only sand and miles and miles of windswept ocean.

(And of course, your family is there, too.)

There is no bullying on the island.

You can walk down the beach and feel the sand in your toes and admire each tiny shellacked toenail, perfect as a shell, and listen to the waves.

There is solitude on the island, and rest.

(And, of course, your family is there, too.)

The island is green.

It does not look like the White House does, like someone

heard the phrase "white Christmas" and thought that it meant all color had been purged from the world and all joy had been forgotten.

It is just green and blue, and it is warm, so warm. You can feel the sun on your face.

(Your family is there, too.)

There are no ballerinas on the island performing only for you, as if you had sleepwalked into a child's nightmare of *The Nutcracker*. No one is performing for anyone. There is no one there at all, so everyone is kind.

(Well, of course, your family is there, too.)

At first you will eat the food you have brought with you, but later you will strike out for the middle of the island to see what bounty it offers. You will find a spring and drink from it, laughing at its coolness.

You will climb a tree and harvest its fruit, and you will sing with the joy of labor. One morning, as you awaken by yourself with the sunrise, you will see a lizard lazing by your foot and for a moment the thought of how it might taste, the crunch it might make as you bite into its tiny bones, will cross your mind. But you will settle back in the sand to sleep.

Your tan will be flawless.

(And, of course, your family is there, too.)

There is color here in the sky—red and blue in the birds' wings, but it does not mean anything in particular.

You use your red hat for fetching water. The writing fades.

Everywhere there is a great stillness.

You catch up on your magazines, but only the most cheerful ones, unhooked from time and the news. There is no cell reception here.

You read: Meghan Markle is getting married. To a prince,

even! That's nice. You feel nothing but happiness for this Meghan Markle, marrying her prince, somewhere in a cold city far away where the flashbulbs paint cages with their tiny lights.

You are alone, at peace, with no eyes to see you but your own, and they will not disturb you again.

And, of course, your family is there, too.

December 8, 2017

The Day
Donald Trump
First Became
a Stable Genius

*Actually, throughout my life, my two greatest assets
have been mental stability and being, like, really
smart. Crooked Hillary Clinton also played these
cards very hard and, as everyone knows, went down
in flames. I went from VERY successful businessman,
to top T.V. Star . . . to President of the United States
(on my first try). I think that would qualify as not
smart, but genius . . . and a very stable genius at that!*

—PRESIDENT TRUMP

WHEN THE AMERICAN PEOPLE VOTED unanimously
to declare Donald Trump a genius (this is what it means to be
elected president on your first try), at first, he did not feel any
different.

The shape of his thoughts in his head felt roughly the same,
and when the sentences formed they did not appear to weigh any
more than they had weighed before.

He was sitting in Trump Tower idly looking over at the book-
case when he suddenly noticed that some of the words on it

were not "TRUMP." He did not remember having noticed that before. Curious, he stepped closer and began to read. One of the books was in German. He loved reading German, he discovered. He loved reading, full stop.

He read all the books, ravenously, so quickly he could scarcely believe it. By 4:00 a.m. he had read everything there was to read in Trump Tower (in fairness, there was not much to read in Trump Tower) and had to call out for more books. Encyclopedias. Histories. Memoirs.

He read them all until his eyes watered and his head ached.

Before, he had felt vaguely confident that if he ever sat down and thought about it, he would probably be able to grasp the concept of special relativity. Now, finally, he sat down and thought about it. He did not immediately grasp it, which surprised him, until he realized that he had to learn the mathematics in which it was grounded first.

By lunch he had it figured out.

He built several ant farms, each with a different model of government, to see which would run the most efficiently. He learned the word "syzygy." He read *Ulysses* and the entire critical apparatus.

"Did you know," he said to Ivanka, when she joined him for lunch, "that the heartbeat of a mouse is 650 beats per minute?"

"No," she said.

"That must be so fast," he went on. "Like a buzz, almost."

"Yeah," Ivanka said, looking a little worried.

✦ ✦ ✦ ✦

No one around him noticed the change immediately.

His team came in and said that he had lots of great ideas and the best brain, but then one of them tried to distract him with what was clearly a maze for a child.

"You have a lot of letters praising your performance yesterday," someone said.

He looked at what she was handing him.

"Those aren't letters," he said, faintly. "Those are—you just printed out some stuff from the website for *Fox & Friends*."

Everyone exchanged a concerned glance, which he picked up on, and he quickly found an excuse to leave the room.

Had the people around him always been so...distinctly underwhelming? Trump wondered. He went to the window and looked down. There were several protesters with signs that contained obvious solecisms. This was a word he understood now.

At least he had Steve Bannon, who was definitely an intellectual. Or he always looked rumpled, which seemed like much the same thing.

"Send in Steve," he said.

Bannon came in, and Trump was excited to finally be sitting there, head to head, with a fellow genius.

But when Bannon opened his mouth, none of the things that came out made any sense.

"Steve," Trump said, "talk like you usually talk."

"I am," Bannon said.

Trump blinked repeatedly. "No," he said. "Usually you sound smart, and now you sound like someone dumped out the contents of some rejected Wikipedia pages onto the floor at random. Speak like Thomas Cromwell, although, ha ha, before the beheading."

"Thomas Cromwell was beheaded?" Bannon asked.

Trump blinked levelly at him, and soon Bannon thought up a reason to go away.

Trump looked over his speeches again.

"Have they always been so...racist?" he asked, quietly.

"What?" Stephen Miller said.

Jared Kushner pushed the door open.

"I am going to solve the conflict in the Middle East," he said.
Trump sighed loudly.

He called for a hot towel and put it on his forehead and went
to bed early.

✦ ✦ ✦ ✦

The next morning was distinctly unpleasant. An aide came in
and turned on his shows, as usual.

A few minutes in, he became agitated. "What is this?" he
kept saying. "This is for imbeciles. Why have you taken away the
intellectually stimulating show I usually watch and replaced it
with this?"

"You love this show," Hope Hicks said reassuringly. "You
watch it every day."

"I can't possibly watch this every day," Trump said. "This is
tripe. Also, why does everyone keep sending me steaks that are
cooked to the consistency of vulcanized rubber? Only an idiot
would order steak cooked that way."

No one made eye contact with him, but that night, for what
they claimed was no particular reason, his entire family showed
up.

"Ha," Trump said, "look, it's a community production of *The
Lion in Winter*." He laughed long and hard. Don Jr. laughed
immediately and Eric did not laugh at all. Ivanka and Jared
looked nervous and exchanged a glance.

"Lion?" Eric said. "Where?"

"It's not about actual lions," Trump said. "Obviously, it's
symbolism."

"SIMBA-lism," Melania said.

Trump looked at her and they shared a brief smile.

✦ ✦ ✦ ✦

His daily routine began to grate on him. All the television and the sitting. There were no books in most of his rooms, and all information presented to him was in the form of pictures. This newfound genius and stability just made him worried and indignant all the time, and none of the food he felt he ought to eat tasted good at all. His people were not what he had hoped. His agenda seemed haphazard at best and misguided at worst.

His head ached all the time. Once he used his excess mental energy to tip over a glass with his mind, but nobody gave him any credit for it. Just for kicks, he raised and lowered the flag on the Interior Department so that it appeared Ryan Zinke was there when in fact he was NOT, but that was not as much fun as anticipated. Everything began to wear on him. He could not sit through international summits. Everyone spoke too slowly.

Gradually he tried to move things that were bigger and bigger. By the end of the first week he was able to knock rockets out of the sky. He sent a tweet about it, but nobody understood that this was what he was trying to say. All the TV ever seemed to show was people closely misreading his tweets. It was miserable. It was a nightmare.

Maybe, he thought, he would wake up and everything would be back to the way it was, and he would still know he was smart without having to see the people who said so. Maybe, if he just used all his brainpower, he could restore the world to the way it was before. Maybe all he had to do was concentrate.

No, concentrate harder. No, harder.

January 12, 2018

Welcome to the Normal, Low-End Furniture Store for Trump Cabinet Members

$5,000: The amount then–acting Housing and Urban Development Secretary Craig Clemmensen said to HUD colleague Helen Foster "will not even buy a decent chair"

$31,000: Custom-order dining table and chairs HUD Secretary Ben Carson has been attempting to cancel

$139,000: Door upgrade at Secretary Ryan Zinke's Department of the Interior

$43,000: Very secure phone installed in Environmental Protection Agency Administrator Scott Pruitt's office

$70,000: Two replacement desks, also in Scott Pruitt's office

WHERE ARE THESE PEOPLE SHOPPING FOR FURNITURE???

HI, AND WELCOME TO A definitely normal, inexpensive retailer of normal furniture at reasonable prices. Thanks for coming in, Mr. Secretary!

First, do you need office supplies? Be sure to check out our pens, which are $800 apiece and made of the shinbones of a saint. We also have cheap, low-end pens (ballpoint, with one color of ink) for $100, if you want to save.

Obviously, we offer a range of very affordable tables and chairs. These really run the gamut! On the high end, we have a saber-tooth tiger leather piece stuffed with an actual member of the middle class. Or you'll probably want one like this—made from that same cheap and reasonable material, but it swivels! Or, if you're desperate to save, on the low end, we have a barely acceptable chair for a mere $5,000. This hideous chair is made from the pelt of only a single snow leopard, and no effort was made to give the snow leopard a classical education.

Over there you can see our range of affordable tables. Our best seller comes directly from Versailles and was briefly used as a guillotine to punish the excesses of the aristocracy. In the midrange, we have one constructed from the trunk of a redwood that grew unmolested in California for hundreds of years, pre-dating the arrival of Lewis and Clark.

Ooh, I see you looking at that conference table. It LOOKS like a normal conference table, but before we put the finish on, we took the entire paycheck of a family of four and burned it in front of them. That's what those streak marks are. Tears, and the residue from the burning. If you spread a cloth on this table and speak the magic words, it will be set with all manner of good dishes and you can feed almost a million people, but that carries an added markup of $150,000.

But if you don't need the cloth or additional features, you can get it for $31,000.

What other items can I help you with?

A phone? We have a range of those, starting around $20,000, pretty much your standard phone price. Our cheapest one is a member of an improv team holding his hand like a phone, and our next cheapest is a different member of the same improv team holding his hand AS THOUGH IT CONTAINS AN INVISIBLE PHONE. Next cheapest is a novelty phone shaped like a banana that does not actually make calls, but it looks so much like a banana you forgive it. Our most expensive phone is a carrier pigeon, but he's very reliable and has a PhD. Or you can get the Very Secure model, which tends to run about $43,000, but it's worth it if your calls are full of SECRETS.

Okay, I see you need a desk. Again, we have a range. At the top of the line, we have the Ramses II, made of rare stone hewed from the tomb of a pharaoh, and if you sit at it long enough, you are guaranteed to achieve work-life balance. Any secretary seated at this desk will obey your demands without question, and their stenography will be perfect. Those who use this desk long enough don't have to spend time in purgatory after they die. The soul of Thomas Jefferson is trapped in this desk. (We can also remove it, but that costs an added $40,000.) On the low end, you can get a desk that is just a white-collar worker with a firm, flat back, braced on all fours. If you get a set of two ($70,000), you'll save $800,000 (the cost of a lifetime of regret incurred by knowing your desk was lonely).

What else? A door? Okay, we have a series of doors. Our cheapest is $100,000. It's not actually a door, just a picture of a door, but the picture was painted by Pablo Picasso. That's expensive for a door, but cheap for a Picasso! Our next cheapest is $102,000. It is a Georgia O'Keeffe painting we think might be a door, but it might also be something different. You need a working door? We have one door that can work *if pressed,* but it was educated for a life of leisure, and sometimes it will just decide not to work for no real reason. It is a very classy door, though, and a charming addition to cocktail parties.

We have a normal door that opens fine, but it's $120,000, and sometimes when you open it, it leads to Narnia and you have to spend decades of your life in a magical kingdom resolving disputes among mythical creatures. For $139,000, we can make sure that won't happen.

Is that everything you needed? Great. I can start ringing you up over here. I'm so glad you came. Don't worry, these prices are all very reasonable—according to Louise Linton. Why, it's barely a single chartered flight!

April 6, 2018

Keep Scott Pruitt Moist

Every good president has a cabinet that reflects his priorities. George Washington had Hamilton and Jefferson. Abraham Lincoln had his team of rivals. Donald Trump has a cabinet comprised of only the best people, including EPA head Scott Pruitt, a man whose repeated demands for his staff to drive from hotel to hotel seizing bottles of expensive lotion for him, among other things, was in absolute keeping with this administration's general ethos and should have raised no further questions.

SCOTT PRUITT MUST HAVE HIS moisturizing lotion.

Why?

Do not ask why.

Scott Pruitt appears to be a man with gray hair. He appears to be a man like other men, though he is charged, unlike other men, with the protection of the environment.

But he is letting the environment change, just slightly. Just enough for another creature to be quite comfortable—one with a hardy exoskeleton that thrives in warmth and darkness.

And Scott Pruitt must have his moisturizing lotion.

NOT THAT ONE! That is an ordinary lotion. The lotion Scott Pruitt requires is quite rare and available only at Ritz-Carlton hotels, and not even *all* Ritz-Carlton hotels. Hurry, we must drive. We must find the lotion. It must be absorbed into

Scott Pruitt's pores. Its scent must travel around him. He must be entirely shrouded in its scent, like Earth by carbon dioxide.

Is it urgent? What will happen if Scott Pruitt is not given his moisturizing lotion?

Have you seen what happens when you leave an earthworm in the sun on hot asphalt? Have you seen what happens to the things that live in a wetland when that swamp dries up? Have you seen a salamander left too long in a hot car? Have you seen a lobster without its shell?

Unrelatedly, we must find Scott Pruitt his lotion.

Scott Pruitt must be seated at the front of the plane, behind the little curtain. Perhaps a private jet would be better, all things considered. It would be safer. None must see what happens when he reaches 30,000 feet.

What will happen?

Nothing, nothing! Naturally.

But it might be good, all the same, if he had a secure door at his office, with a biometric seal. A door that only he may open, that will recognize him, even if—

Do not ask, "If what?" Drive! We must find the lotion. Scott Pruitt must be kept moist.

It is not that Scott Pruitt is beginning to assume a new and monstrous shape. It is of course nothing like that.

Scott Pruitt is trying to keep Earth warm. As it becomes warmer, he will need more ointment and another mattress. In fact, he needs the mattress now. It is a very particular mattress. It could accommodate an enormous exoskeleton made entirely of cartilage. Scott Pruitt is certainly not terraforming Earth to be warmer and stormier and filling the air with smog.

On an entirely different topic, Scott Pruitt must have a secure door that responds only to his touch.

The rectangular bottle in which the lotion is kept is dangerously low. And if Scott Pruitt does not have sufficient moisturizer—

And we must find Scott Pruitt a mattress. Not any mattress. One mattress in particular.

What is it that he needs them for? What will happen if he is not kept moist and his back is not properly supported?

Do not ask. Drive, drive!

He must have a soundproof phone booth in his office. No sound must escape this booth, not even the cracking of a hideous and enormous exoskeleton. Not even the sound of moisturizing lotion being frantically slathered on the creature within! Not even its bellowing—a bellowing too loathsome for human ears. We must keep him secure.

Drive, drive! Get the lotion!

And aides must pay for these hotel rooms. That much is clear. The taxpayer must not question. The taxpayer must understand that this is worthwhile. The taxpayer must know that some things are too terrible to behold.

Are you saying that if, for a single night, Scott Pruitt were not kept properly moist, with access to a mattress that meets certain exacting specifications, something terrible would befall us?

Think if they did not meet these specifications. Think what might emerge from that $43,000 soundproof booth. Think what might escape that $5,700 biometric lock. No, never mind, do not think of it. You must not think of it. You would go mad.

Drive, drive! Put on the flashing light on the motorcade, if you must! Drive, drive! Scott Pruitt must be kept moist. We must keep him moist at any cost.

July 5, 2018

I'm Beginning to Suspect These Were Not, in Fact, the Best People

WELL, GOSH. THIS IS EMBARRASSING. I promised my team would be the "best people," and, wow, it looks like maybe that was not the case. It is turning out, that, in fact, the people surrounding me and filling this White House were not at all as advertised! Or maybe exactly as advertised! I am starting to notice this from all the trials that keep happening.

I thought I had the best team ever to be assembled, but I had a big coat full of skunks, six rejected concepts for Batman villains, and a disembodied voice that yells rude things in the Quiet Car.

I thought I had the finest cadre of advisers and lawyers the earth had ever seen, but now that I look I see that all I had was the Ghost of Christmas Yet to Come, an aardvark in a Model UN sweater, a hairpiece on top of a novelty skeleton with light-up eyes, a Mr. Monopoly Man, a paid advertisement for unscientific vitamin supplements, and a cursed Oscar statuette brought to life until someone speaks the single phrase that will allow him to sleep once more.

I had a white supremacist—just full stop; three reverse pictures of Dorian Gray; what should have been a complete set of the two door guardians from a logic puzzle (one always tells the truth and one always lies), but the first one did not arrive with the rest of the shipment; an enormous wind sock attempting to sell used cars; and a shark disguised as a meter reader. I really should not, in retrospect, have put two hand-puppets from a wisely canceled local-access children's show in charge of a Cabinet department, and I definitely should not have been taking legal advice from a half-hour-long program in which Pat Boone urges you with increasing intensity to buy sixty-eight CDs from the 1950s.

I thought I had the best people, but I had a big plane filled with money, a bear that has wandered into a school by mistake, zombie James Buchanan, a pair of Ivanka Trump pumps that want to speak to a manager, the hair of a televangelist, a Pixar villain whose origin story involved a tanning bed struck by lightning, and an anthropomorphic liver. I had a scorpion asking for a ride across a river; an ominous forwarded email with a sad face drawn on it; a statue brought to life by the love of its sculptor, but, in a twist on the classic Pygmalion scenario, it was a Confederate statue; a piece of toast on which sexist words appeared for no reason; a gallon container of snake oil in an expensive leather coat; everyone at a surf-side bar on a Thursday; a reality-TV contestant; and Anthony Scaramucci.

I am chagrined. I thought that a pick-up artist book in a big-collared shirt, an animatronic statue of Rutherford B. Hayes reprogrammed by HYDRA, and the Thing that appears in the mirror when you blink were good people to surround yourself with, but, in fact, no. A television chicken sales personality, a stand of reeds into which hateful words have been whispered for months, a bag of money with a severed finger in it, a book by a Fox News personality brought to life by the love of a lonely child and a phrenology head—not the elite team I had been led to suspect!

These were not, I now realize, the best people. I get this sense from how frequently they keep being forced to quit, getting charged with and admitting to crimes.

Look, if Melania Trump's campaign has proved anything, it is that nobody knows what "Be Best" means. But somehow I feel like it is not this. I am quite let down! Next time, I will be more specific.

August 23, 2018

HOW DARE YOU DO THIS TO BRETT KAVANAUGH?

Now it is time to turn to the period of unpleasantness surrounding the confirmation of Brett Kavanaugh to the Supreme Court—a time many recall less-than-fondly, doubtless because they were forced to watch the nightmarish spectacle of a man briefly afraid he might not get exactly what he wanted.

HOW DARE YOU?!

HOW DARE YOU DO THIS TO BRETT KAVANAUGH?

HOW DARE YOU DENY HIM THIS SEAT?!

Listen—NO, YOU listen!

Do you know who Brett Kavanaugh is? Brett Kavanaugh went to Georgetown Prep!

BRETT KAVANAUGH IS AN OPTIMIST WHO LOOKS ON THE SUNSHINE SIDE OF THE MOUNTAIN!

If Brett does not secure a lifetime appointment on the Supreme Court, this country will be IN SHAMBLES! THIS IS HIS BIRTHRIGHT! Do you know how embarrassing it is for a Georgetown Prep graduate to NOT be on the Supreme Court? They are literally 12 PERCENT of the court! THIS IS PROBABLY THE WORST INDIGNITY YOU CAN INFLICT ON A HUMAN BEING!

ALL BRETT IS ASKING FOR IS DUE PROCESS! DUE

PROCESS BEFORE HE IS DEPRIVED OF HIS GOD-
GIVEN RIGHT TO A SEAT ON THE HIGHEST COURT
IN THE LAND, WHERE HE WILL DETERMINE THE
FATES OF MILLIONS!

Apply the standard you want to apply to your husband-
brother-son. He should be allowed to be careless. He should be
allowed to like beer.

BRETT LIKES BEER!

WHO DOESN'T LIKE BEER!

BRETT ISN'T YELLING!

YOU'RE YELLING!

YOU SHOULD BE ASHAMED!

THIS IS BRETT'S SEAT!

The Founders did not break from Britain so a landed white
gentleman accused of sexual misconduct could NOT be put in
charge of something!

ARE YOU GOING TO BELIEVE HER, AMERICA?
OVER HIM, AMERICA?

YOU HEARD THE WOMAN! SHE DOESN'T EVEN
LIKE TO FLY! YET SHE FLEW HERE! SHE DOESN'T
REMEMBER ALL THE DETAILS OF THE EVENING,
WHEREAS HE KEPT A CALENDAR, LIKE HIS FATHER
BEFORE HIM!

HE IS NOT EMOTIONAL!

YOU ARE EMOTIONAL!

NO, YOU LISTEN!

If this is how you are going to behave, if you are going to
believe this woman, if you will let her stand there and destroy
his life (well, not his life, technically, nor his freedom, just his
chance of a seat on the highest court in the land), then what kind
of country is this going to be?

They are going to drag him here in front of all these OTHER MEN and deny him a seat on the Supreme Court, and he will have to walk home confused and disoriented, and he will have to live with the feeling that he is NOT ON THE SUPREME COURT for as long as he lives.

This is OPPRESSION! TO BE DENIED POWER OVER OTHERS! IF THAT IS NOT WHAT IT IS, DO NOT TELL ME.

The right to decide what happens to other people is one a man like him is born with, ONE OF THOSE INALIENABLE RIGHTS, AND IT SHOULD NOT BE TAKEN FROM HIM WITHOUT BEAUTIFUL DUE PROCESS!

NOW HIS WORLD IS FALLING APART! NOW HE IS BEING FORCED TO GO OVER HIS HIGH SCHOOL BEHAVIOR WITH A FINE-TOOTHED COMB! THIS IS NOT FAIR! THIS SCRUTINY! THIS DEMAND TO ACCOUNT! HE DESERVES THIS POWER! GIVE IT TO HIM! STOP ASKING HIM THESE QUESTIONS!

STOP SAYING THINGS! SHHH! BE QUIET! STOP RESISTING BRETT KAVANAUGH. STOP TRYING TO STOP HIM.

NO, LISTEN! LISTEN!

HE DESERVES THIS!

LISTEN, YOU DON'T DESERVE THIS. AMERICA DOESN'T DESERVE BRETT KAVANAUGH ON THE SUPREME COURT.

IF THIS IS HOW AMERICA IS GOING TO BEHAVE, IT DOESN'T DESERVE BRETT KAVANAUGH AT ALL!

September 27, 2018

The FBI Has Been Very Easy to Reach about Brett Kavanaugh, and Of Course the Report Has Been Quite Easy to Read

Even before the investigation ended, several people who said they had information that could be useful said they ended up mired in bureaucracy when they tried to get in touch with the FBI.

—THE WASHINGTON POST, *OCTOBER 4, 2018*

The FBI's report is available at a sensitive compartmented information facility, or SCIF, in the Capitol Visitor Center, a secure room designed for senators to review sensitive or classified material, two Senate officials said. Just one physical copy of the report is available, and only to senators and 10 committee staffers cleared to view the material.

—THE WASHINGTON POST, *OCTOBER 4, 2018*

Hɪ!

We hear you have information to share with the FBI about Brett Kavanaugh! We have streamlined the tip process as much as possible in hopes of getting right to the bottom of this.

With that in mind, please call the indicated hotline. The person who picks up will direct you to a dedicated drop box, in which you will find a crumpled sheet of paper with GPS coordinates, which will guide you to an underground vault where you will encounter a hanging sword and a flask. (You will not be able to lift the sword until you take a swig from the flask.)

Once you have entered and swigged from the flask, grab the sword and hide behind the door to the vault. When the troll who dwells there returns home, strike off all three of his heads at once. You must strike the three at once, or they will grow back, and the FBI will not be able to contact you.

In a hollow tooth of the troll's third head is a key. Use the key to unlock the inner door of the vault, where you will find a telegraph machine, with a telegraph operator slumbering over the controls. She alone can transmit your message, but to awaken her, you must find and blow three blasts on the silver horn that hangs just east of the sun and west of the moon in the heart of the glass mountain, which is a castle.

The glass mountain (which, again, is a castle) is easily reached by whatever mass-transit project is under construction in your area. Ride it to the end of the line, then go to the bathroom. Stand there a day and a night until, in the other stall, you see two pairs of feet that do not look like human feet. Knock three times on the partition. If the creature with two pairs of feet that do not look like human feet does not knock back, wait for it to leave, then go home without ever looking behind you, and thank whatever gods you worship that you escaped so easily. If it knocks back, come out. This is your steed.

Do not look it directly in the eyes, or I cannot say what will befall you. Climb on its back and ride until you come to the house of the North Wind. The North Wind will pose you a simple riddle to make certain you are approaching the FBI in good faith. Do not be alarmed by the many skeletons of those who failed to answer the North Wind's riddle! This has caused problems for people in the past.

When you have answered the riddle, the North Wind will give you a golden spindle. Something similar will happen when you reach the house of the South Wind, who will give you a golden skein of yarn, and in the house of the West Wind, where you will be given a golden ball. Now your steed will take you to the glass mountain on the back of the West Wind.

Stand outside and play with your golden spindle. An old crone with a pile of paperwork will approach you. Tell her you will give her the golden spindle if she helps you complete the paperwork. Her sister will come to see what is happening. Her sister is the custodian of the polygraph machine. Do not give her your yarn until she lets you access the machine. The final sister holds the key to the glass mountain. Give her your golden ball.

Enter the glass mountain, looking neither to right nor to left, and you will find the silver horn. Your steed will bear you back to the vault where the telegraph operator slumbers. Blow three blasts upon the horn, and when she awakens, tell her what you know. She will send your information to the proper authorities, where it will be processed as soon as it is received, by an agent who will whisper your information into a reverberating cave of echoes hundreds of meters below ground that will keep whispering it forever.

Oh, you wanted it to reach the Senate? Then I have no idea.

See also: "Directions for Accessing the FBI Report (During the Blood Moon If You Approach the SCIF Not Walking and Not Riding, Not Hungry and Not Full, Not by Day and Not by Night, in Alternating Shifts of an Hour by Party)"

October 4, 2018

You Are in Melania Trump's Nightmare Forest of Cursed Red Trees. Keep to the Path.

LISTEN TO ME. THE TREES in the White House were all green when I got here. They were all green as recently as Monday. But the trees have *turned*.

Walk faster.

Don't be afraid. The trees would smell it.

Things are wrong here. Little details are wrong. The attorney general is different. He hasn't been confirmed by the Senate. We go nearly a month between daily press briefings. The trees are red. The phrase "Be Best" is everywhere. "Be Best." As though to "be best" is grammatical and not the clumsy articulation of a child. But there are no children in the forest. This forest is no place for children.

Last year the trees were a hideous, ghastly white. It was always winter and never Christmas.

This year everything is red. It is perfectly natural that the trees are red. The trees are red (the Internet says) as a handmaid's cloak. Do not think of blood. Keep walking.

Has anyone seen or heard from Scott Pruitt? Don't look startled. Has anyone seen or heard from Jared Kushner? Do people even remember that there is such a person as Jared Kushner? Then what does his voice sound like? Can you remember ever hearing it? Keep walking. Look straight ahead.

You are all right. Keep to the path. Walk between the trees. Keep your face relaxed.

Do not look down the hallway, where someone appears to have been dragged a great distance and there is a wreckage of tiny red needles. It was only the grabbers. Let it be. Clutch only your White House Christmas ornament. You may hear something that is not quite a heartbeat. Walk on.

Outside the White House you will hear the great murmuring, the women in their hats, crying, "Mueller shall deliver us." The litany goes up. The supplication echoes. "Mueller is coming to change everything. Everything will be Revealed. Nothing will be suffered to be hidden. The trees will crackle and burn in his magnifying glass's purifying flame."

Do not listen to the forest's derisive laughter. Keep to the path.

Staffers have wandered into the forest and not come out. You must count the trees as you pass them to keep to the right way. The angles are—I do not know how to put it—they are *wrong*.

If you keep walking and do not count the trees as you pass them, sometimes you will come across Jeff Sessions making a pair of dainty shoes, working his tiny hammer and adze so deftly that you can scarcely believe your eyes.

Or you will happen upon the hut deep in the forest that stands on chicken's legs and plays *Fox & Friends*. It wants you to come in. It has a cooking show. Don't go in. It is not a cooking show. You know what it is.

Deeper still in the scarlet wood, Matt Whitaker awaits in a chalet made entirely of Muscle Milks. Standing sentry is the Rat King. He will ask you to dance. He will ask to appear on a panel at your festival of ideas. You must keep walking.

You must count the trees carefully. The eleventh tree is a Mistake. Do not look at it. Do not let it enter your imagination.

If your eyes alight upon the tree, transported, you will stumble upon the Mueller indictments in a clearing, cold and still. But it is not their time! At your footstep they will unseal, scream, and become dust before your eyes. Then it will be only stillness. You will be alone in the forest, and no one will come for you.

Keep to the path.

November 28, 2018

Lock Her Up?

Do you remember where you were on this day?

ALL THE BELLS CLANGED IN every port, in every steeple of every church. As the somber knell rang out over the entire land, President Trump sat motionless at his window, gazing out over the countryside.

"You know the penalty, my lord."

He nodded. He knew the penalty. That was why the bells tolled.

All the flags slid all the way to the bottom of the staff. A velvet drapery was placed over every statue, even the good ones he was annoyed the states were trying to replace. Around the neck of every ox, a small bell rang mournfully with every step.

What could the nation do but weep?

In the towns they began to rend their garments. The plowmen at their plows doffed their soft caps and threw them to the ground and trampled upon them. The valleys were still, and the glens and dells, but if you listened you could hear the faerie folk lamenting, and a mournful tinkling as many tiny bells began to ring out. The oceans halted momentarily in their rise.

All the shoes everywhere were placed into a pile and burned. All the books, too, but that was unrelated.

Limo drivers began weeping and could not continue. Limo passengers unclamped their chains of pearls and let them spill to the ground. In the gas station coffee shops, disgruntled voters telling reporters they felt left behind fell silent.

The city streets were empty. A child whispered a question to his mother and was quickly hushed. All the mannequins in the shop windows were denuded of their Christmas garb and clad in solemn black. Times Square was dark and still.

"It's time now, sir."

President Trump did not turn from the window.

She had done it, the one unthinkable crime. Even she, his only daughter (except Tiffany). The most awful crime a person could commit. Indeed, there were no other crimes. The one thing! The one unforgivable thing!

She had sent government emails from her private account.

If justice were to remain in the land, any semblance of justice, she must bear the punishment. They must begin the chanting.

"Couldn't we just . . . decide we didn't actually care about this?" he asked.

"Impossible! We cannot be safe until all such evildoers are eradicated!"

Ivanka waited, surrounded by her handmaids, her head shrouded in a veil, for the sentencing.

He turned with a heavy sigh. "Lock her up."

Across the nation, from rally to rally, the chant joined the rolling of the bells. He did not watch as they led her away.

———————

November 20, 2018

My Book Report on
The Mueller Report

After many months of intense effort, Special Counsel Robert Mueller produced a report. And people definitely read it.

I ENJOYED READING *The Mueller Report*, a book that contained 448 pages, each more exciting than the last, as well as more than 1,000 footnotes! The book was published in 2019, meaning it is relevant to our times, and it contained many themes and symbolism, which I will explain in the course of this report. At the back it also included a list of characters. Some people just skimmed through this report to come to conclusions they already had, but I did not, as this report will show.

The Mueller Report is about a man who wanted to find information, but really, I think, what he found was the American Dream. It is exactly like *The Great Gatsby*, a book about a man who pretends to have more money than he actually has and turns out to owe everything he has to sinister forces but for whom you ultimately feel pity because he is lonely even though he has a big house, in that both books are about a narrator who is trying to find out information about one thing and ultimately discovers something else.

Basically, the American Dream is elusive to lots of people, and some people would say that it does not exist at all, which is also what people in this book say about collusion, which shows parallelism.

One theme of *The Mueller Report* was that it contains 448 pages. That is a lot of pages, and it is very impressive to read a book that long, as, of course, I did. But many of the words are covered up in thick black bars, which makes the reading go fast because of pacing. I would argue that the bars are even a character. In the writings of Kurt Vonnegut, a large asterisk drawn in thick black ink stands for a part of the human body. I am not sure what part it would be in this book.

The colors red, green, blue, and white also recur repeatedly throughout this book. Green symbolizes spring, renewal, money, and envy. It can also symbolize Personal Privacy. Yellow symbolizes cowardice. It also refers to portions of the book that deal with Investigative Techniques, but I think it can mean both things at the same time. Red is usually blood or anger but here alludes to the Grand Jury, whose presence was felt throughout this book.

This whole book is an example of synecdoche, in which a part stands for the whole. For instance, you say "wheels" when you mean "a car," or "the unredacted portions of *The Mueller Report*" when you mean *The Mueller Report*. Synecdoche is a useful rhetorical device and I like it a lot, even if it is not one of the ones Winston Churchill mostly used.

The conflicts of Man vs. Man and Man vs. Society are very prominent conflicts that are demonstrated throughout this book. Sometimes, a character will find himself opposed to other characters, who will try to stop him by just not doing what he has asked or by pretending they are confused by his request or sometimes by resigning. The Deep State, in this book, can represent society.

One way in which this book did not succeed was its lack of

female characters. Ivanka Trump appeared briefly, but her character was not as developed as it could have been. Hillary Clinton was, in some ways, the villain of this book, according to some, but I think if it were their intention for her to be the villain, they should have made her do more. They just say she is crooked without stating why, which is an example of telling without showing.

Throughout the book, the character of Donald Trump was looking for protection, which we see from the fact that the word "protect" occurs more than eighty times in the course of the book, although some of those times, I am now realizing, are at the top of the page next to the title of the report. But mostly they are in the text. He wants protection, which is demonstrated by him saying, " 'You were supposed to protect me,' or words to that effect" to Jefferson Beauregard Sessions III, whose name is a telling reference to lost causes.

This book examines the theme of protection through all three types of irony. In his quest for protection, Donald Trump makes an allusion to the play *Angels in America* when describing what a good protector should do (not take notes, just like Roy Cohn). This is an example of verbal irony. Secondly, the character Michael Cohen also says he wants to protect the president, but some characters disagree that this is what his actions accomplish (situational irony). And lastly, when Donald Trump says, "I'm f—ed," it is an example of dramatic irony, because he does not yet know that Congress is going to protect him and never take any action that could possibly lead to him not being in office anymore, which is something we as the reader already know.

A character I really liked was George Papadopoulos, who was referred to as "Greek Guy" in a footnote to show comic relief. It is good to have some characters whom you do not have to take seriously, especially if the book is long.

The narrator seemed very ambivalent. Sometimes I thought, am I supposed to trust this narrator? Sometimes the narrator seemed on the verge of saying something very profound, but then there would be another black box. Black boxes can also symbolize censorship.

I found the black boxes distracting but also moving. This book asks, in a way, are we not all trapped in boxes, unable to connect? I think the boxes were very indicative. Sometimes the box looked like a Tetris that was successful, as on page 44. Sometimes the box looked like a brutalist beret. I think the boxes were a kind of Rorschach test for the readers to see whatever they are inclined to in them. I saw the craven darkness at the heart of everything. This is like in the famous book *Heart of Darkness*.

Also they symbolized the American Dream.

One thing that I liked about the book was that it let you draw your own conclusion about what people's motives were and whether they were wrong to do what they did. I think it will be fun to discuss that part a lot.

I did not identify with any of the characters in this book.

I would recommend this book, in spite of how it ended.

April 18, 2019

You Think Trump's Getting Impeached? I Defy You to Convince Anyone at This Cursed Truck Stop.

YOU THINK YOU'RE GOING TO find support for impeachment, do you? You dare suggest that this presidency is embroiled in chaos? Well, I am at a truck stop right now to wait out an electrical storm, and nobody here agrees.

I've been interviewing for what I figure is at least an hour—the clock on the wall is broken—and everyone I speak to still supports the president just as much as they did the day he was elected. They are happy to say so, even if it means talking to folks like me on a daily basis.

The old man at the end of the counter shakes his head when I tell him the president is beleaguered by scandal. He's not tied to his phone, like some of you coastal types. He's not bound even to the latest fashion. I notice he's wearing an old wide-brimmed hat and rimless spectacles, the kind I haven't seen outside of movies. He says he's still with the president, and that he doesn't pay attention to the daily buzz of news. He has priorities like many real Americans have.

I want to go out to my car, but it's raining too hard. Coffee here is only a nickel. I order another cup.

I try to say something about the impeachment, but no one can hear me over the noise of the soybeans, growing healthy and strong. I have never heard a soybean so loud before. Here, we have our priorities straight, straight as the corn growing just outside the window. I can't see my car.

The TVs here aren't tuned to CNN or MSNBC for the scandal of the day. No, sir. They're playing what appears to be Rudy Giuliani chanting an uninterrupted mantra for the past six hours. When I look at my watch, the hands don't seem to move, but when I look at it again after my next sip of coffee, it says hours have passed. How long have I been here?

Someone tries to mention the phone call to the president of Ukraine, and out of nowhere, pigs in all the neighboring fields begin to screech, horribly, an almost human sound, and they only stop when he gives up mentioning it.

The storm is still going.

You might think Donald Trump is mired in scandal, but here at this diner, we don't agree. We like to see the media get riled up. The corn and soybeans don't care about what the president has been doing on his phone calls to Ukraine.

Whenever I try to ask, something rustles against the window, and it's corn. I think it must be higher than an elephant's eye now. The corn is pressed right up to the glass. I think the corn wants to get inside.

There's a Norman Rockwell painting hanging on the wall, and it says it doesn't think the president has done anything bad. There's a scarecrow in a pair of dungarees with a big pitchfork. He and his pitchfork both voted for Trump. They will vote for him in the next hundred elections. When I turn around from talking to them, I don't see the windows anymore. Is it day or night? I thought there used to be windows. Has it always been so dark? Are we underground?

The waitress refills my coffee.

Do we even have foreign adversaries? I forget.

At this truck stop, no one has a reflection. It is 2016 here, I think. Joe Biden has done something wrong. Joe Biden has done something very wrong. Hillary Clinton had better not win. If she wins, the country will be broken for good.

I can't see out the not-windows at all. I think we're definitely underground now. The walls are packed earth and so is the clock and it still hasn't moved and now there is something crawling in the wall.

The wall bursts! There's an enormous worm here, and I pledge allegiance to it, willingly. I burn my notebook for King Worm! We are burning everything.

My arms are now guns. Everyone laughs. This is our joke together.

We don't care about a single thing that President Trump has done since taking office. We are not ashamed to say so. We love the Kingdom of Saudi Arabia. We love the stock market. There's a crude drawing on the wall of a stock market going up and up, but it doesn't have a scale indicated on it. I don't remember coming here.

Real America Doesn't Care About This Trumped-Up Scandal! Real America Doesn't Care About Any of This! Giuliani's voice chants and chants and reaches a crescendo and the radio chants with it. We are here in the heart of America! The walls squeeze in and out, like the clenching of an enormous fist!

Something somewhere is screaming. Maybe it is the something that used to be me. I feel calmer than I ever have. The scandals don't touch us here.

September 26, 2019

Part II

ROUTINE NIGHTMARES AND SOOTHING FABLES

IF YOU HAVE A NIGHTMARE OFTEN ENOUGH, IT becomes more disturbing to go to sleep and not find the nightmare there. At a certain point the nightmare becomes home. At a certain point it is stitched underneath your skin. If it were not for the nightmare, you might not be certain it was Thursday.

Who are we to say that these are nightmares? They are too familiar. These are perhaps not horrors at all, but features of the landscape, geysers that spout forth scalding, sulfurous steam hourly, like clockwork.

No, these are not nightmares. These are simply stories we tell ourselves to illustrate more fully the beautiful intricacy of our matchless world. The hideous sound you hear now is a lullaby.

It Is Very Difficult to
Get the Train to Stop

*I was . . . wondering whether I would just be jumping
in front of a train that was headed to where it was
headed anyway, and that I would just be personally
annihilated.*

—CHRISTINE BLASEY FORD,
*ON WHETHER TO COME FORWARD DURING
THE KAVANAUGH HEARINGS*

I AM SO TIRED.

The train is very, very urgent. It is moving a man's career forward. It is very difficult to get the train to stop.

The presumption is that the train will not stop. The presumption is that you will be a scream thrown on the tracks. That it will require a great many of you to be thrown onto the tracks before the train will grind to a halt. It can never be just the one; it must be several at once. Someday we will know the precise conversion. We will tell them: Do not bother unless there are twenty others like you, because the train will continue, and you will be crushed.

It is painful to watch a woman caught and torn in the gears of a man's progress. To watch the meaning of her name change into a thing that happened to her once. To watch the first sentence of her obituary get rewritten. To watch her name be linked to this man's name (Anita, accuser of Clarence; Christine, accuser of Brett). All she asks is for the train to stop.

To make the train stop, you must throw yourself in front. Your whole self. Your fear of flying. Your family.

You must throw yourself in front of the train, but still it may not be enough. These trains move very fast. We must not ask why.

Maybe the train will stop for a week. That seems fair. A week, just to make sure. A week, to take this seriously, at a gentleman's request.

But I am so tired.

I am so tired of this constant parade of pain.

In the Bible, Thomas says he will not believe that Jesus has survived unless he can stick his hand into the wounds. But this is not a reasonable thing to ask of someone who is not God, to stick your hand into their wound. I am tired of watching people become wounds. Half the Internet is a wound. Have you stuck your hand in it enough? Do you believe yet? The #MeToo movement lurches forward over a path of scars. The change is so slow and the sacrifice it demands so great.

Even as she testified Thursday, Christine Blasey Ford kept apologizing. ("I'm sorry," she said. "I can read fast!" she said. She was here to be "helpful," she said.)

Someday I want to not be tired.

Someday I want us not to apologize.

Women are used to squinting to see our own stories in the stories of others. To reading ourselves into the words "all men are created equal." To being the thing tied to the tracks to raise the stakes.

I am so tired of the moment when you discover how little your weight counts against the train's.

I want us to be the train and not the thing thrown under it.

I want us to be the thing too urgent to be stopped, not the thing that must curl up apologetically to make room for it.

Is it too much to ask to be the train sometimes? Not all the time, just sometimes.

I am so tired of watching us jump.

I am so tired of watching the trains keep going.

September 28, 2018

A Humanizing Profile
of Your Local Neo-Nazi

ARE WE DOING THESE? OKAY!

One thing that may surprise you to learn about Neo-Nazis is that they live in houses! You would think that maybe one would live in some kind of enormous bone hut, or a stack of burning newsreels, or a large tent constructed entirely from problematic flags, but actually no. Actually Henrik (whose last name I am withholding, for some reason) lives in a regular house. With a two-car garage, where a tennis ball hangs on the end of a sturdy rope as a caution to those who want to move forward too far. Henrik immediately drew an analogy from this ball that I don't want to repeat! But amazingly, the tennis ball is there in his house, just like in other people's houses. It doesn't just corrode away the moment he touches it. WILD!

Strangely, in pictures, Henrik appears in full color, not sepia-tinted or wearing a little pickelhaube. This surprised me very much.

It surprised me less, but still a little bit, to learn that he has a dog and that the dog is just as loyal to him as a dog would be to a regular person. I don't know if the dog understands all of his beliefs. The dog sits at his feet and he pets it and scritches it behind the ears.

Henrik and I go to a Putt-Putt golf course. He puts on a shirt that expresses his beliefs, just like it's a normal shirt. But it's not a normal shirt! The shirt says some pretty impolite things. Wow! And yet: He puts it on one arm at a time! And his head goes through the hole at the top, just like a regular person's head.

When he hits the ball, no talons come out, and when he retrieves the ball from the hole, he does not shiver away into dust! He likes art and music, not just Wagner. He also loves Hatecore. He said it isn't a contradiction to love Hatecore. He acts like "Hatecore" is just a genre of music, like other genres! I'm so confused.

His lights turn on and off, with a light switch. Can you believe this guy?

On the surface, Henrik is a striking young man, with a sharp and well-delineated chin and eyes that seem to open the windows to his soul. His eyes (and soul), like the lives he thinks #matter, are blue. When he stands next to the exposed brick wall of this coffee shop in excellent lighting for my photographer to snap pictures, he crosses his arms. I ask why he is crossing his arms. Is he trying to keep people out?

Yes, he says. Keeping people out is actually his thing, politically. Also, he thinks it looks metal. Which, honestly, it does.

His shirt is off-white, as he hopes America soon won't be. He is wearing a belt with a buckle, which isn't like anything, but it's a very fetching belt.

How do I put this? Like many regular people, Henrik is a LOOKER! At least an 8, a number I am told he appreciates more than some numbers but less than others! Just like people! I'm losing my mind here!

He has a girlfriend! WHAT? Can you believe this guy? I can't believe this guy. Just like people! Is this even allowed? He's so—what's the word?—mundane. But also another word that I won't remember in time for this article.

He has a computer, not, as I had kind of expected, an ENIGMA machine, and he is busily typing away on it, just posting his words and videos on the Internet with other people's words and videos, like they are just the same. People might see them and think these were things that a person, living today, with a dog and a garage with a tennis ball, thought! He voted for the president! When he isn't rallying or posting hate-filled screeds, he likes to go fishing, and sometimes he even catches fish!

Once someone did not serve him at a chicken restaurant, he says, and it made him very unhappy, almost as unhappy as one time when he went to a playground and saw little children judging one another by the content of their character.

We sit down. He thanks me for being here, for taking this time with him. He wishes more people would see him as a person. Just like he also sees *some* people, but not everyone.

Now Michelle and Ivanka Are Neighbors

Jared Kushner and Ivanka Trump moved to a house in Kalorama—less than two blocks from where the Obamas reside after vacating the White House. Here, naturally, is what ensued from such proximity.

AT THE OBAMA HOUSE in Kalorama, a Secret Service officer rings the doorbell. Another Secret Service officer answers. After a brief period of negotiation, Ivanka Trump appears on the doorstep with a casserole. She is wearing an impeccable blue sheath dress and her hair has been blown out in long, beachy waves. "Hey, neighbors!" she says, in a pleasant, low voice. "I brought a casserole. I hope that we can be friends."

"Thanks," Michelle says.

"Also, Chelsea and Al say hi."

"Chelsea . . . Clinton and Al . . . Gore?" Michelle asks. She cannot help noticing Ivanka's shoes: black kitten heels made of a shiny patent leather. They look fantastic.

When the door shuts behind her, Michelle and Barack smile at each other. "She seems nice," Barack says.

"I loved her shoes," Michelle says.

The casserole is delicious. Between themselves, the Secret Service, and the girls, they finish the whole thing.

The next day, Michelle takes back the pan.

Ivanka greets her cheerily at the door. "Come in," she says. "I hope you liked the casserole."

"We did," Michelle says. "You know, if you need to talk about anything—climate change, maternity leave—I'm always here."

Ivanka beams. "Do you really mean that?" she asks. "That means a lot."

Michelle nods understandingly.

"I do have one thing I want to talk about," Ivanka says. "I heard you go to SoulCycle. Do you like it? I've been meaning to try."

"You should come," Michelle says. "Let's move!"

"Really? I'd love that." Ivanka pauses and taps something on her phone. Her nails are shell pink and perfect.

"Really."

Ivanka puts the phone away. "Sorry," she says. "Just posting on Instagram."

"Of course," Michelle says. "Where's the bathroom?"

Ivanka points.

On the way there, Michelle trips over a pair of shoes. Beige heels, suede, with a rounded toe. They have Ivanka's name in them. Even as she trips over them Michelle cannot help remarking on their beauty.

When she gets back the TV is playing CNN and it says that Donald Trump has just tweeted something highly alarming. Ivanka smiles apologetically and shrugs. "We can't choose our families, can we?"

That afternoon Michelle goes through her closet, on a whim. One of her favorite pairs of shoes has Ivanka's name in them. She would never have noticed before but now she is starting to see the name everywhere. Ivanka Trump. IT.

When she checks the closet again, there is another pair. But she must have miscounted.

After they go to SoulCycle, Michelle finds a gift box on the front doorstep.

"From Ivanka," the Secret Service agent says.

She opens it. It is a sheath dress, impeccably tailored. It is so nice. She is about to put it on but something in the mirror catches her eye. A pair of heels in the hallway. She doesn't remember leaving them there, but she must have. They are black and strappy and made of smooth patent leather. She puts them back in the closet and shuts the door, feeling suddenly cold.

They start to see each other as a matter of course. Whenever Donald is on TV, Michelle notices, Ivanka merely watches and says nothing. Her face is perfectly calm and unreadable, like an Instagram picture of a porcelain teacup.

Barack does not think anything of it, but it lands funny in the pit of Michelle's stomach.

The next week, Michelle goes to visit a friend.

"Is it weird living next to Ivanka?" the friend asks.

"No," Michelle says. "She's nice."

"That's good to hear," the friend says. "I love her clothes. And you can't choose your family, can you?"

Michelle's foot touches something under the table and she looks down. It is an exquisite pair of beige heels (the tag says "nude," but they are beige). For a moment it seems as though they are watching her, but that cannot be right.

Michelle dreams that when she puts on the sheath dress, it catches fire. Everything is on fire. Ivanka sits in the White House and smiles.

She wakes up, panting. The lights in the house down the block are still on. It is not that the house is watching her. There is nothing out of the ordinary about the house. It is not that the house is waiting for her to make a false move and then it will snap.

"Have you ever seen them talk at the same time?" Michelle asks.

Barack sets down his seventh almond of the evening with a pointed clink. "Michelle," he says, "you need another project. I think you're getting cabin fever."

"I've never seen them talk at the same time," Michelle says. "I'm just pointing it out."

Michelle has started going to SoulCycle at odd hours, but it is no good. Every time she looks in the mirror she is aware of Ivanka behind her, cycling madly, blond ponytail bouncing. Something about it feels wrong.

When she gets off the bike she turns around to say hi, but Ivanka is not there.

"I hear you're neighbors with Ivanka," one of her SoulCycle friends says in the locker room.

Michelle nods.

"She made my purse," her friend says, voice low and confidential. "I was going to boycott all Trump products, but—I think she's one of us. And you can't choose your family, can you?"

Michelle feels as though a cold hand has seized her by the wrist. For some reason her locker will not shut. When she looks more closely she sees that there is a stray shoe: a sleek, blue patent-leather flat, reasonably priced and beautifully crafted.

"Is this yours?" she asks.

"No," the friend says. "But what a great shoe."

Whenever they go out to friends' houses, even friends who object to Donald, Michelle looks around the house and sometimes she sees the shoes, two or three of them, peering out from under a chair or the bottom shelf in a closet.

She stares in the bathroom mirror that night getting ready for bed, thinks of mentioning it to her husband. But "I think Ivanka Trump's shoes are following me" is not a thing a sane person would say.

She sees Donald Trump leave the house but she never sees him enter the house.

She tells this to one Secret Service agent and the agent nods and looks concerned but later she sees her talking to Barack when they think Michelle is out of earshot.

Ivanka invites her over for macarons and absentmindedly taps something on her phone. Michelle looks down at her own phone. Donald Trump has just tweeted.

"Just posting on Instagram," Ivanka says smoothly. Her eyes are watchful. "I like your shoes!"

Michelle looks down and gasps. When she left the house she was wearing Louboutins. She knows this. But on her feet are delicate white leather kitten heels with a splattered floral pattern.

"Thank you," she says.

When she gets home she tears them off and sits against the wall of the closet, panting. IT. Stephen King was right.

"Have we ever seen him tweet?"

Barack looks up from where he is slicing carrots. "Michelle."

"Have we ever actually seen him tweet?"

Barack tries to massage her shoulders reassuringly but she pulls away.

She gets into a car with her Secret Service agent and asks him to drive her to a certain location in New York.

Bill Clinton is at home. She rolls the window down and yells. "Where's Hillary?"

Bill shrugs. "I don't know," he says. "She's taken to the woods."

Michelle gets out of the car and continues on foot. Her heels slow her down. She does not think she was wearing heels when she left the house. She tears them off and runs.

Hillary sits in the forest surrounded by a circle of elegant white leather flats. Michelle throws them aside and Hillary looks up at her as if awaking for the first time.

"You knew," Michelle says.

Hillary nods. "She had gotten to Chelsea by then. We never stood a chance."

When she gets home, the Secret Service agent tells her that Barack has "gone to see the neighbors" and she walks down the block with a leaden sensation in her chest.

When she arrives there is no sign of him. Ivanka answers the door before she can ring the doorbell.

"Michelle!" Ivanka says. Her mouth smiles but her eyes don't. Michelle is never sure what color her eyes are. "What a lovely surprise! Please, come in. I'm making macarons."

"Barack?" Michelle calls. "Barack?" She walks inside. The door shuts behind her.

Ivanka walks to the kitchen. Michelle stands frozen, a sudden terrible certainty congealing within her. She opens Ivanka's Instagram and scrolls and scrolls. There is no mention of politics anywhere. Every post is Ivanka, impeccably attired. Ivanka and her children. Ivanka at a podium. And the timing on the posts seems funny. Scheduled, even.

She hears footsteps: lovely robin's-egg-blue heels, moving ever closer, clicking on the hardwood floor.

"Do you want a macaron?" Ivanka calls.

Michelle must get out of this beautiful house. She tries the doorknob but it doesn't turn. If she weren't extremely fit, she would be breathing hard.

"Everyone has two theories of Donald Trump, don't they?" Ivanka calls, pleasantly. The heels start down the hallway. "One, that he is awful and the other, that he can't be that bad, because—look at his family. Look at Ivanka." The footsteps are closer. "All right. *Look* at his family."

Michelle tries another doorknob. But none of the doors is the right door. The next door opens but it is a closet. On the floor lies something like a human skin. It is orange and topped with a curious tuft of hair. It looks like a pool inflatable from which all the air has been released. Its blue-gray eyes stare beseechingly up at her. It begins to puff up, slowly. "She exists to show them that they are safe," its low, belching voice says. "But no one is safe."

"It's you," Michelle shouts. "You are not a prisoner of this family. You are this family."

Ivanka smiles. It is the same nice smile as ever. "Try getting them to believe you."

The door at the end of the hallway is open and Michelle is running. But it keeps getting farther and farther away, and there are shoes in the way. So many beautiful shoes.

January 6, 2017

Why Won't This Career Die?

Charlie Rose Will Reportedly Host a Show About Men Brought Down by #MeToo

—THE CUT

Matt Lauer Is Planning His Comeback

—VANITY FAIR

Louis CK's Path to a Comeback Likely Runs Through Comedy Clubs

—THE HOLLYWOOD REPORTER

PANTING WITH EXHAUSTION, she let the stake drop from her hands. It was done. She had made her Allegation public, spoken the Killing Words, and the Man's Career was dead.

This, at least, is what everyone had said.

"Do you understand what you're doing?" they had wondered, anxiously. They knew—centuries of lore, from those who had sought to destroy a Man's Livelihood before, had warned them—that merely hinting at some sort of scandal would be enough to destroy a Promising Gentleman's Career for good.

She had felt bad. If there were a way to punish only the Man. The Career had not been always and entirely bad, and she had been a little sad to be the agent of its destruction.

But it was done. She had killed it. The worst was over. She heaped dirt and garlic on it, bleeding and exhausted, and began the long trek back.

◆   ◆   ◆   ◆

The first weeks were pleasant. She went out to coffee with people who told her of her bravery. They asked her how she was enjoying her new fame.

"What fame?" she asked. (She had gotten three emails that day, but none of them were from admirers; they had been disciples of the Career, and they swore vengeance.) Someone had knocked her mailbox off its post. She spent about half an hour reaffixing it, checking all the screws to see that they were secure. For a split second, as she closed the flap, she thought she heard the Career laughing.

◆   ◆   ◆   ◆

She felt bad for the Career. It was not the Career's fault, the things the Man had done. The Career had been a source of joy. It was like a delicious sausage of whose precise ingredients she had been unaware; she could not deny that it was tasty, and maybe there was nothing wrong even in the meat itself, but once you learned that the only person able to make it ate a baby's arm each time, nothing about the taste changed, except your awareness of what it meant to be a person who liked that taste.

Sometimes, at night, she thought she heard the Career whisper that it was coming, but she was sure it was only the wind around the house. Only the wind.

✦   ✦   ✦   ✦

They had said the Career was dead, but it wasn't dead.

They had shunned her as a murderer. She saw her own Career wither and die. But at least the thing was gone and it would not trouble anyone else.

The first twitches were noted less than a month afterward. Someone in an interview had said he missed it, and for a moment she thought she had seen it twitch. But that was nothing, they assured her. She had murdered it (MURDERER!), and it was dead.

Only it wasn't.

✦   ✦   ✦   ✦

She came home and her child was drawing something. It emerged slowly in firm swipes of the crayon beneath her little girl's stubby fingers. At first it looked like a monster with spaghetti for a head. There was something unshakably ominous about it. Something she almost recognized.

"What is that, sweetie?" she asked, her voice shaking a little.

"It's an inevitable comeback tour," her daughter said. "Do you like it, Mommy?"

She swallowed down the sickly sweet taste of bile in her mouth. "You did a very good job with the coloring," she said. "What made you decide to draw that?"

Her daughter shrugged, starting on a new picture that appeared to show the spaghetti-headed monster being given an award of some kind by its peers. "It's only a matter of time, Mommy."

✦   ✦   ✦   ✦

She was startled to see it on the cover of a magazine. She blinked and it was still there. The Career. Bloodied and grinning.

"Never," they had said when she pronounced the fatal words. "Never again."

She showed the magazine to a friend.

"What?" the friend asked.

She pointed at the Career in horror. "It's winking," she said. And the word next to it was not "never" but "when." In precise and clinical terms the article explained exactly how it would come back and when you might expect to see it return. When.

"How?" she asked.

✦   ✦   ✦   ✦

She got home late one night and her Doberman was choking. She could not tell what it was choking on. She grabbed her little girl and the dog, and they took him to the vet together.

The vet stared at them with horror and pulled a finger out of the Doberman's mouth. Around the finger was wrapped a head-line indicating that Charlie Rose planned to help kick-start the Man's Career Resurgence. She screamed and screamed, but her daughter merely observed the images with a deadly calm.

"Everyone deserves a second chance," her daughter said, "don't you think, Mommy?"

✦   ✦   ✦   ✦

She spoke the words again, but the words did nothing. The Career kept lurching closer and closer.

Her daughter's teacher asked whether she had meant to put An Important Man's Career on the designated pickup list at school.

"No," she said, her stomach churning. She rushed to the

school and grabbed her child. She could see it everywhere now, coming closer and closer. Whenever she looked behind her, it was there. Every time she blinked it came closer.

She approached a roadblock and a whole sea of undead Careers came lumbering out of the earth, toward her. They came crawling down off billboards and magazine covers, their jaws hanging cavernously open, the hideous skeletons visible. They shambled nearer and nearer. She took her daughter in her arms and began to run. Her lungs were raw, like a skinned knee. Her heel broke and she stumbled on, gasping, but the Careers continued. They could not move so fast, but they had all the time in the world, and they were undeterred by obstacles.

✦ ✦ ✦ ✦

As she ran, her heel broken, stumbling in the dirt, she saw another young woman preparing to speak the Words that would end a Career.

"Think what you are about to do," everyone around this woman was saying. "You will kill it. You will murder an innocent Career. What you are about to do is unthinkable, and it cannot be undone."

That was when she began to laugh. Wildly, hysterically. She started to laugh and did not stop laughing. She was still laughing when it got to her.

April 27, 2018

Raising Baby Hitler

The New York Times Magazine *discovered, by polling its readers, that 42 percent of them would kill Baby Hitler. That just goes to show what* New York Times Magazine *readers know.*

I HAVE OFTEN FELT THAT most of historical Hitler's difficulty stems from a life spent constantly fending off assassination attempts from the future, an effort that doubtless left him paranoid and exhausted. Do I have proof for this? Well, no, obviously, but it *seems* right, doesn't it?

Frankly I think if you are going to go back in time and interact with Baby Hitler, you should not kill him. You should try to raise him right. Here's how.

1889

You get out of the time machine and tip the driver. It is April 20 and you are in Braunau am Inn, Austria (yes, Austria! Hitler was Austrian, Mozart was German, as Germany is always reminding us). You are in the Hitler nursery. There is baby Adolf cooing to himself in a lacy outfit. "Yes," you think to yourself. "This is doable."

You pick up Baby Hitler and rock him soothingly back and forth.

A man and woman (his parents, you assume) rush in and start yelling excitedly at you in German. You had forgotten about them. Also, you do not speak German. When you accepted this mission you forgot to take this into account. You put down Baby Hitler, who is now crying something awful, and begin to gesture. "Achtung!" you say. "Achtung!" (You don't know any German at all and you are not sure of what achtung means, other than that it was a U2 album title.) "Ein!" you yell. "Zwei, drei! Quatre! Cinq!"

Mr. and Mrs. Hitler are now more concerned than upset. Mrs. Hitler picks up little Adolf and soothes him. You try the time-honored American method of speaking English loudly and slowly in the hope that suddenly people in a foreign country will miraculously understand you.

"Mr. and Mrs. Hitler," you say, slowly, "I would like to take this baby and raise it for you. You see, your son here grows up to become the worst dictator in history, responsible for mass genocide, but I—" (well, this sounds really stupid now that you're saying it out loud, but I suppose you're stuck) "—feel that I will be able to do a better job raising him than you did."

Mr. and Mrs. Hitler speak excitedly to one another and you assume that they are saying something along the lines of "Come into my house and say a thing like that! You really think it's my parenting that did it? I'll have you know I'm going to have two more children who will not grow up to be world dictators!"

You see your opening, grab little Hitler, and make a break for it.

The next eighteen years are the most stressful of your life.

AGE: ONE

Baby Hitler is teething and it is driving you up the wall. Does it still count as traveling back in time heroically to kill Hitler if you do it because it is 3:00 a.m. and Baby Hitler has awakened you from your first sound sleep in weeks? He's still probably going to be a genocidal maniac, even if you have been playing him a special record called *Music Definitely Not by Wagner* to put him to sleep every night.

AGE: TWO

Baby Hitler is now Toddler Hitler. The only thing worse than the terrible twos is knowing that the toddler currently dragging you through the terrible twos is Adolf Hitler. Tiny Adolf manages to eat a knob off one of the cabinets. He smiles knowingly at you as he does it. You become very upset and take away his Soffee Giraffe, which you brought from the future because everyone associated with it said that it was the One Toy Guaranteed Not to Screw Up Your Baby in Any Way.

Toddler Hitler throws a tantrum that reminds you of the worst excesses of his speaking style later. "Adolf," you tell him, sternly, putting him into his I LOVE GREAT BRITAIN, AND I WOULD NEVER ATTEMPT AN AIR CAMPAIGN AGAINST IT lion pajama onesie, "if you carry on like that, no one is going to listen to you or take you seriously."

AGE: FOUR

You drop Young Hitler off at kindergarten. You put apple juice in his lunchbox and make sure all his snacks are kosher so he can share if he makes friends. You hope he makes friends. His early childhood felt interminable but now it seems like it's gone in the blink of an eye. He is wearing his favorite sweater with a giraffe on it.

AGE: FIVE

Young Hitler brings home a drawing he has made. "That is a beautiful drawing," you tell him. "Unless my telling you that this is a beautiful drawing will make you believe that you are a great artist and then later you will be rejected from art school and it will warp your psyche, in which case, no, it is not a beautiful drawing."

"Thank you?" Young Hitler says, uncertainly.

AGE: SIX

Hitler makes a friend, Kyle. You ask him what he wants to do after school and he raises his hand and shouts "SEE KYLE!" and you faint dead away.

AGE: EIGHT

Hitler says he needs a bigger bedroom because he requires more "living space." "WHERE DID YOU LEARN A THING LIKE THAT?" you ask, panicked. "THAT IS A COMPLETELY ERRONEOUS IDEA." You try to send him to his time-out spot but then panic that you are associating territorial restrictions with punishment. Instead, you announce that you are going to read Nietzsche to him. ("Nietzsche is always a punishment," you say, "not something people voluntarily read.")

AGE: NINE

Hitler drinks chocolate milk and it lands in an unfortunate pattern on his upper lip. You panic. Otherwise uneventful.

AGE: TEN

Hitler brings you a mug that says UBERMOM: WORLD'S BEST.

"I am not better or worse than other moms," you explain, nervously. "All moms are equal."

"Whoa," Adolf says. "Okay. Geez."

AGE: ELEVEN

"We had a career fair at school today," Adolf tells you. "They asked what we wanted to be when we grew up."

You freeze. "And what DO you want to be when you grow up?" you ask, nervously. "Remember, you can be anything you want. The sky's the limit. Just not a horrible dictator who kills millions of people. Unless, by putting that off limits, I make it the one thing you want to do. Wait, never mind. Pretend I didn't say anything."

AGE: TWELVE

Hitler asks if he can walk to school by himself. You panic. Without the Internet to tell you whether you are parenting right or not, it is difficult to tell what approach to take. Is Helicopter Parenting or Free-Range the right approach to take for a growing Adolf? Should you send him to camp this summer or not? Does he need a math tutor? Would being better at math help or hurt him in the long run? Why didn't you think about any of this when you decided to take this on?

AGE: THIRTEEN

Hitler has written a report for school entitled "My Hero is Abraham Lincoln." You go through it with a red pen correcting Hitler's grammar.

"There should be a word for someone who cares as much about grammar as you, Mom," Hitler says.

"There is," you say. "A grammar n—Lorax. A grammar Lorax."

Age: Fourteen

Hitler gets a growth spurt. One morning he comes downstairs and announces that he is trying to grow a mustache. "Absolutely not," you tell him.

Age: Fifteen

Hitler has been locked in his room all afternoon and you don't know what's going on in there. "You need to let me in, Adolf," you say, knocking for a fifth time.

"SHUT UP!" he yells. "YOU DON'T KNOW ME! YOU DON'T KNOW MY LIFE! YOU DON'T KNOW MY STRUGGLE!"

"I WISH YOU WOULDN'T USE THAT WORD!" you yell back.

Age: Sixteen

You should not have thrown Hitler a Sweet Sixteen, but he asked so nicely. He gave a speech, but it was bad. He looked at his shoes the whole time and mumbled and spoke indistinctly. This made you feel pretty good.

Age: Seventeen

Hitler doesn't get into art school. You cook him his favorite dinner and repeat the family mantra, "Other people are not to blame for your problems." He seems okay but he is so hard to read these days. Teenagers.

Age: Eighteen

He gets into college and you ride there with him. There are so many lessons you wanted to impart. But what can you possibly say now? You hope he packed enough sweaters. He outgrew the one with a giraffe on it years ago but you still have it in a drawer.

"Don't worry, mom," he says. "I'll be fine." But will he? You don't know.

You leave him at the dorm and cry all the way home. Maybe you should have killed him when you had the chance.

October 23, 2015

You May Already
Be Running

WHEN YOU WENT TO BED, you were a senator or a governor or a representative.

It had not touched you yet.

But now it is 2019.

You wake up in a cold sweat with only one thought: Somehow you must get to Iowa. You are not from Iowa. But it is calling to you. You think, "If I do not get my hands around an ear of corn, I will perish. If I do not clutch an Iowan infant in my arms, something horrible will happen. If I do not tell the people of Iowa what I think is wrong with America—and yet, what I think is right with America, too—then life will no longer be worth living."

You have been to Iowa maybe once or twice before. You thought nothing of it at the time. You saw John Delaney there, out standing in his field. He heard the call before anyone else. He dropped his plow and let his oxen run free and went straight to Iowa. You laughed at him.

But now you must get there. You must get there this year. You feel the stirring in your blood. There is something there for you, and you must go.

People asked you, "Are you thinking of it?" And before you said no.

Now you are "not able to rule out thinking of it."

Once the idea has insinuated itself, it is only a matter of time. Even the act of not thinking about it admits the existence of the possibility of thinking about it, and by then, it is too late.

Suddenly, your life begins to change.

You have written a book. You did not know you were writing a book until you saw it at the airport one morning with your name and face on the cover. (When was this picture taken? You do not remember taking the picture.) The book is called *Uplifting the Dreams We Hold Dear*, or *My Country 'Tis of Thee*, or *Sweet Land of Liberty*, or *Certainly We Must All Promise*, or *Every Day Is Extra!!!!*, or *This I Swear*, or *God Dreamed a Wish*, or *Six Things I Know*, or *I Dreamed a Dream*, or *Life Worth Living*, or *A Fight We Must All Fight*, or *We Had Better Fight*, or *We Hold These Truths*, or *To Be Self-Evident*, or *That All Men Are Created Equal*, or *And Endowed by Their Creator*, or *With Certain Unalienable Rights*, or *Among These, Life*, or *Liberty and the Pursuit of Happiness*, or *My Uncle Made Me Swear to You This Day*, or *My Grandpa Made a Promise*, or *Neighbors*, or *United*, or *Divided*, or *Stronger*, or *Scrappy Little Nobody*.

You flip through the book. It has a very wide font. You have discovered a lot of things wrong with America, the book says, but also a lot of things great about America. You wish someone existed who could solve some of them and celebrate others of them.

You find yourself sitting down with party leaders. Why? No reason. Can't you sit down with party leaders? Can't you go to Iowa?

You feel a great urge to prayerfully weigh the question. You find yourself having a conversation with your spouse about how best to serve at this time. You feel the need to consult with your family. You consult with them as you have never consulted before. Are they ready for this, you wish to know. They must be ready. The last thing your spouse said at the conclusion of your last candidacy was "IF WE EVER DO ANYTHING RESEMBLING A CAMPAIGN AGAIN, I AM MOVING TO A BUNKER IN CANADA AND TAKING THE CHILDREN." But did your spouse wish to be taken seriously, or literally?

You begin to listen for what the people want. What is America crying for? You must be ready to listen if America starts to cry for you specifically, say by forming a PAC in your honor.

Your opinions grow vaguer. Someone asks what you think about Medicare-for-all, and suddenly you find yourself supplying a vacant answer as though you had never heard the words "Medicare," "for," or "all" before and are making up your own definition at random.

People asked before, "Are you running for president?" And you said no. Now you say, "I am not not not thinking about it. I am beginning to consider the possibility. If the people ask."

The urge is strong upon you. You are like a salmon trapped below a dam. You cannot stay here any longer. You must go somewhere to better hear the people. To consider and mull, you and your family, together. To not rule things out. You must go to Iowa.

January 2, 2019

The Privilege Tree

ONCE THERE WAS A PRIVILEGE TREE and it loved a little boy.

And the boy played under the shade of its thick canopy, and the tree protected him.

One day the boy was hungry. "Tree," said the boy, "I am hungry."

"I know what to do," the tree said. "Go to the corner store and steal some candy and run back here to me."

And the boy did. He filled his pockets with candy and ran back to the tree as quickly as he could. The man who owned the store chased after him, but when he saw the boy beneath his tree he shrugged and said, "Boys will be boys." And there were no consequences, and the tree protected him, and the theft did not go on his permanent record. (For, after all, he was just a boy.)

The boy grew older. "Tree," said the boy one day, "I am bored."

"I know what to do," the tree said. "Pluck one of my branches and carve it into a toy gun and wave it around. That will amuse you."

And the boy did. And the tree sheltered him under its thick leafy canopy of privilege and everyone who saw him shrugged and said, "Boys will be boys." And there were no consequences, and the tree protected him, and no one even thought to telephone the police. (For, after all, he was just a boy.)

And the boy grew older still. "Tree," said the boy, "I must leave for college soon, but I am bored."

"I have an idea," said the tree. "Pluck my fruit and ferment it and drink its juices." And the boy did, and while he was under the influence of this fermented fruit he did something terrible.

He ran to the tree. "Oh no," the boy said, "what have I done? Do you hear what she is accusing me of? I will surely have to face consequences now."

"Nonsense," the tree said, ruffling his hair with its leaves. And from its thick canopy of privilege the tree produced a lawyer and a big pile of paperwork to discredit the boy's accuser and point out what a shame it would be for the world if the boy's promising athletic career were to be derailed.

And the judge in the case saw the boy sitting under his tree and shrugged, "Boys will be boys." (For the judge himself had once been a boy with a Stanford tree of his own.) And there were no consequences, and the tree protected him.

And the boy played beneath the tree and had all kinds of glorious adventures. He rolled up the leaves of the tree and put funny things in them and smoked them, and he drove his car twenty miles above the speed limit, and as long as he took shelter beneath the tree, everyone shrugged and said, "Boys will be boys." And there were no consequences, for the tree protected him.

"What a wonderful world this is!" the boy cried. "How wonderful I am!" He tore off several of the tree's leaves and began to write a novel, which was very well received.

And the boy grew older and taller still. He went away to a faraway land and made merry and urinated in a gas station and tried to claim that he had been robbed at gunpoint.

And the boy ran for his tree as fast as he could, but its thick canopy was very far away and without the shelter of the tree everyone could see that he was not a boy but a thirty-two-year-old man and they wondered why they had allowed things to go on for so long.

But when he reached the shade of the big tree he looked so small and pitiful that they shrugged and said, "Boys will be boys." They apologized to *him*, and there were no consequences, and the tree protected him.

And many years passed and the boy committed a white-collar crime. And the tree was still there, although it was beginning to rot from within and several people with sharp axes had come and stared at it in a dubious manner. "Boys will be boys," the tree whispered, "and besides, the details of this crime are quite boring and technical." And the boy faced no consequences—or very few.

And the boy grew very old and so did the tree. One day the boy heard his tree creaking in the wind.

"What is the matter, tree?" the boy asked. "Are you all right?"

"No," the tree said, and shivered. "I am not. Trees like me should be for children, not grown men. Look." And the tree pointed, and the boy saw for the first time that there were not many trees like his still standing. "I ought to have been cut down long ago."

"Cut down?" the boy asked, and for the first time in his life the boy was frightened. "But then what will happen to me if I do something wrong?"

The tree shrugged. "The same thing that happens to everyone else," it said. And the tree groaned and fell.

And the boy saw that the world was not quite so wonderful when you could not shelter anywhere better than a Reasonable

Doubt Shrub (which is nice, but nothing like a Privilege Tree). And the boy saw that it was not he who was wonderful, but his tree, which had protected him for so long, without his realizing it. And the boy, at last, grew up.

Some say.

August 19, 2016

Part III

THIS
FOLLOWS

YOU MAY WELL BE THINKING, "HOW PLEAS-
ant it is to live in a world so blandly normal, so
absolutely dull." And you are right. This world holds
no surprises. The voices you are about to hear are
just logical, expected parts of life in the present—
things that follow naturally from the established
rules of our beautiful universe. There is nothing disturbing about them, because they are so routine and
ordinary! These are things we have now, definitely.
These are just things that we all know must happen,
in accordance with the way we know the world to
work. This all follows.

Also, this section comes after other sections.

Excuse Me, Director, I Have Some Questions About My Role in the Spring Play as a Crisis Actor

After the Marjory Stoneman Douglas High School shooting, many students spoke out in favor of gun control—and certain very specific parts of the Internet accused them of being "crisis actors" hired for the occasion. Naturally, crisis actors would require a crisis casting.

Dear Mr. Spencer,

First, I am SO excited to be cast in the spring production this year as a crisis actor, and I look forward to giving the role my all! Since I have previously starred as Courtney (*Legally Blonde*), Chorus (*Grease*), and Factory Worker 3/Third Alternate for Madame Thénardier (*Les Mis*), among other roles, you know you can expect 100 percent commitment from me, even though I am only a sophomore.

As an actor this gives me what I have always craved the most: total anonymity, no attention whatsoever, and a guarantee that no one will ever learn my name. My mom is always like, "Why do I have to drive you to the theater three nights a week, and why can't you go out for track this semester?" and I'm like, "Because NOTHING, Mom." She's supportive, though. I have hinted that I am making great connections. I know that you are connected globally to a large network that literally pulls all the strings of the world, so I am wondering if after this you could get me onto Broadway or at the very least Off-Broadway.

My mom has not asked about the big bag of gold bullion that I have in my room, but she wants to know if I'm really being utilized to my fullest extent, and upon reflecting on it, I have some suggestions to make about my character.

I think the role of Crying Girl with Sign is actually the heart of the production and we overlook this at our own risk. I am already off book (no big deal; I am very devoted to my craft), and I have some ideas about how to expand my part. Right now, I am instructed to cry while holding a sign, cry while not holding a sign, and then, into a microphone, say, "I'm not a crisis actor."

I was thinking I could say into the camera, "I'm NOT a crisis actor," and then I could wink, add, "Courtney, take your break!" and then do a split. I can do a full split. I didn't do it in auditions but usually I can.

I could also say, "I'm not a crisis . . . I'm an actor" in a voice. I can do a number of voices: old woman, Lucille Ball, something that sounds like an old-timey newsman, and sort of a Grover-Yoda hybrid. My voice is my instrument! It is just one of the many arrows in my acting arsenal.

Another thought that came to me was that I could rap the line. "I'm not / a crisis / or a member of ISIS / I'm an ACTOR!" but obviously I'm not Lin-Manuel Miranda. (I WISH! Once he favorited a tweet that I did where I sent him a drawing of himself as a crab and it was honestly the best day of my life, not to boast.) But if you like the idea, I can write a longer verse. I am a triple threat! Not in the sense that anyone is in danger from me, just in the sense that I act, sing, and dance. Obviously no one is in danger.

Damien Tucker is going to be amazing in his lead role as Articulate Person that Part of the Internet Will Become Very Suspicious Of. If you want us to be in any scenes together I AM VERY READY. In my mind, Articulate Person that Part of the Internet Will Become Very Suspicious Of and Crying Girl with Sign have a long history together, and I can act with my face and body—or do a dream ballet!—if you do not think this merits another line. We could even KISS right before he says his line (do not tell him I suggested this).

I also want to know if you plan to do anything about the fact that Laura Jenkins never says her line right. I am not confident in her ability to cry on cue (when I was Factory Worker 3 and she was Fantine, I noticed that she brought a damp sponge with her backstage right before "I Dreamed a Dream"), whereas I can cry at the drop of a pin; I'm literally crying right now as I type this.

I cry easily just by imagining—what if this weren't a play? What if this were real? What if there actually were seventeen dead kids and teachers, but some people were so in denial that they decided it would be easier to imagine a whole cast of children being paid to be crisis actors than have to confront the world we live in? Maybe I'd never stop crying.

Thanks,
Amy

P.S. I could also sing the line.

Everything You Wanted to Know About Deep State But Were Too Scared to Ask

We have been hearing more about the Deep State lately. It is about time. I have cherished my admissions letter to DEEP STATE ever since it was flown down my chimney by an old bat with large leathery wings shortly after my eleventh birthday. It is below.

Congratulations on your admission to DEEP STATE!

We'd love to learn more about you as you make up your mind about whether to attend this elite institution and join the many graduates who proudly proclaim our Latin motto, "status in statu."

First, a question. There are only two ways that ~~muggles~~ Real Americans find out about American Deep State. How did you?

(a) I read an article on Breitbart.com

(b) I am the president of the United States, with access to the work of the world's most vital intelligence apparatus, privy to all kinds of classified information that

can get to the heart of things, and I read an article on
Breitbart.com

We can't wait for you to join the ranks of the Moles. (The mole
is our cherished mascot. Look for him around campus! If you
see him, he has failed in his mission and will be immediately
destroyed.)

Deep State, like Hogwarts, is a secret shadow institution
that exists, invisibly, beneath and alongside everything you
know about and see. All the creepy murals that used to deco-
rate the Denver Airport and fill innocent travelers with suspicion have been rescued and restored and grace the halls of Deep
State. Immediately on arrival, all Deep State students are sorted
into one of four houses: Slytherin, Slytherin, Slytherin, or the
Unelected Bureaucracy of the State Department.

At Deep State, you will learn to warp the fabric of reality so
that you can conduct a secret conspiracy to manage a coup d'état
that is Nixon-Watergate all over again but will also be immediately visible to anyone who reads the *New York Times*.

At Deep State, your roommate could be anyone: a journalist,
an unelected bureaucrat, an Ivy League elitist, a K Street lobbyist,
a Silicon Valley type, a retail associate, a member of Congress, a
paid protester at that very congressman's town hall—anyone! We
appear to be working at cross purposes, but at Deep State, there
is no such thing. These are all parts of Deep State that make us
who we are.

What is the aim of Deep State graduates? A very clear and
very secret thing, only known to Deep Staters and the people
who leave comments on conspiracy websites online.

Do you have any fun campus traditions? Every night before exams we go streaking across campus and then gather in a darkened council chamber to choose a new secret direction for the United States, which we all work to achieve in tandem through a system so secret that no one is told about it or knows what it is.

Do you have any rivalries? Our only rival is the legitimately elected government of the United States. Except Congress, which is a part of the Deep State somehow. It makes sense once you accept it. Also we are rivals with Duke, because nuts to Duke.

What or where is Deep State? Deep State is everything and nothing.

Is Deep State exclusive? Many people do not even know they are part of Deep State.

Do you have any famous alums? We have ONLY famous alums.

Does Deep State offer scholarships? No.

Are speakers welcome on Deep State campus? Unlike regular college campuses, which only disinvite conservative speakers, Deep State disinvites ALL speakers.

Does Deep State have a football team? No, but it controls the outcome of all football games.

Where, who, or what actually is Deep State? It goes all the way to the top.

Who is part of it? All stable institutions everywhere. Not Steve Bannon, as he is neither of those things.

What is it actually? I think I've made it very clear. The Deep State network is extensive, and we have Deep State grads in many fields: Congress. The judiciary. The mainstream media. Global corporations. Think tanks. The State Department. K Street lobbies. The executive branch. The legal complex. Hedge funds. Madison Avenue. The defense industry. DARPA. Army, Navy, Air Force. Pentagon. Intelligence: CIA, NSA, DIA. Department of Energy. Transportation complex. Energy complex. Research universities. Ivy League schools. Silicon Valley. Special Forces. Foundations. NGOs. Retail, banking, mortgages. Wall Street.

All of these careers are part of the Deep State. "Wait, is anything NOT part of Deep State?" you may be asking. Finally, you get it!

After you discover the Deep State, you can access it by going to Platform 9¾ at the State Department and running very hard, headfirst into one of the walls. You may or may not go through the wall, but after a head injury of that magnitude, everything about the Deep State will make sense.

All best, and congratulations,
Barack Obama
President of Deep State

Some Classic
Episodes of
Trump's Space Force

*Space is a war-fighting domain, just like the land,
air, and sea. . . . We may even have a Space Force,
develop another one, Space Force. We have the Air
Force, we'll have the Space Force.*

—PRESIDENT TRUMP

(Swelling orchestral music) Space. Force. The final frontier.
Force. These are the voyages of the space ship *SpaceForce Ship*. Its
continuing mission: to explore strange new worlds. To seek out
new life and new civilizations. To carry the values of the Trump
administration to infinity and beyond. To boldly go where no
one has gone before.

Episode 103: The half-alien first officer explains that because
of his different cultural background, he experiences the world
differently than the captain does. The captain becomes upset—
"I didn't join Space Force so people could lecture me with this
political correctness!"—and makes him leave the bridge. While
this discussion is distracting everyone, the ship flies into an
asteroid and everyone aboard is killed.

Episode 104: The science officer very carefully explains—using a holographic presentation and small, simple words—that diverting all power from the life support to the Space Drive will kill everyone on the ship. The captain gives the order anyway. Everyone on board is, as predicted, killed.

Episode 105: The captain randomly reassigns the ship's doctor to become head of engineering, because he places no value on expertise. No one knows what they are doing and the second there is a problem, the ship explodes and everyone on board is killed.

Episode 107: One of the women complains about the low-cut, skimpy uniform Space Force obliges her to wear. No one listens to her and nothing changes.

Episode 109: A planet is being slowly suffocated by its own atmosphere. All the scientists on the planet have suggested a simple step that will prevent this from occurring and the planet's leader beseeches the captain to help. "Ah, but what if it's not?" the captain asks. The planet implodes, also destroying the ship in the process.

Episode 201: The ship is charged with brokering peace in an interplanetary dispute that has raged for centuries. Space Force is supposed to transport an aging diplomat who has made the study of this controversy his life's work and who alone possesses the rare cultural artifact that will help settle their enmity. But the captain's son suggests that he could do it equally well, probably, because he once saw a video about it, so they put him in charge instead. It does not go well. In the B Plot, the ship gets destroyed.

Episode 301: The ship receives a distress signal from a planet in crisis. The ship ignores it. "We have enough of our own problems," the captain points out.

Episode 304: The captain is given access to a new, planet-destroying weapon. Everyone advises him not to use it because the carnage will be unthinkable, but he thinks it might be cool just to see what it does. The entire bridge crew resigns in protest. He uses it. The carnage is unthinkable.

Episode 310: The entire crew is replaced with children. No one notices.

Episode 401: The ship flies through a wormhole into a Mirror Universe where they all have beards. Everything is incredibly well run, and the work environment is warm and respectful. They figure out a way to return things to normal, but nobody wants to go back, so they pretend they didn't.

Episode 405: The captain is stranded on a planet with people who speak only in metaphors. He becomes frustrated with them and shoots them. They were trying to warn him of a danger threatening his ship, and when he zooms back aboard, the ship instantly explodes.

March 14, 2018

Welcome to AP U.S. History! Everyone Say Hi to the Tank and the 150 Heavily Armed Men.

In the wake of another shooting, someone came up with the glorious idea that teachers could earn bonuses by toting concealed weapons into their classrooms. Indeed! Schools have been soft targets too long. Below, words from a pioneer of the program.

No, Charisse, you cannot go to the bathroom; the armed escort is still in there with Tim.

I also have some personal news: To receive a bonus, which I sorely require, I am carrying a concealed firearm in a pocket holster, which is why my cardigan is draped in such an unusual manner today, and it's also why, when I tripped and dropped the box of pencils that I paid for out of my own pocket because our supplies budget was cut, I clutched my hip and screamed, "OH GOD, NO!" I promise that this will not happen again. I am going to get comfortable with the new requirements for being a teacher, because I think what I do is important, and because the man with strong muscular arms and impeccable aim who would replace me thinks the Trent Affair is something you have outside your marriage with the lead singer of Nine Inch Nails. Ha ha, dating myself there.

The reason I have written "execrable debacle" on the board is because those are two SAT words I would like for you to learn. No other reason. I am sorry that you only get half a textbook; I tried to suggest that those should be a budget priority, but it did not fly. But we did receive funds so that Ms. Clifford—the art teacher—could get three weeks of boot camp and six pistols, and so that a man can stand outside the auditorium with a rocket launcher.

We will not have any active-shooter drills because the president thinks they are demoralizing, unlike the conditions in which I am now going to attempt to teach you about the liberties we hold dear—oh God, what's happening? Oh sure, Tony, I guess it must be hot in the tank. You go ahead and open that top up. I just got a little startled, but it's fine, we're fine. Hoo boy. Okay. We're fine. We're fine. Everyone's fine.

To the members of the security team: You are welcome to take the final, but when I call on people, I am going to prioritize current students.

And remember, we're here to learn! Think of this as a fun mnemonic for the Bill of Rights. When you look around at what we are being asked to do here rather than attempt any sort of restrictions on gun ownership, you may well think, "This is a big pile of number two." And, hey, that's the amendment!

This class is heavy on the reading, and we are going to move quickly through history to get to the present. Although, really, why rush? Look where we wound up.

February 22, 2018

Part IV

MODEST PROPOSALS AND OTHER COMMENTARY

AH, THE MARKETPLACE OF IDEAS! COME TO this wonderful bazaar and inhale a deep whiff of all the magnificent flavors that have been prepared for your delectation! These are the ideas that are best and strongest! They have beaten all the other ideas that tried to stand against them. They have stabbed them with their long, forked tails and bellowed with triumph. You will be very pleased with these ideas, which are the best of their type and smell delicious! Yes, these are ideas that are thriving! These ideas are the best! It is good to hear them. None of them are parodies.

A Good Time to
Talk About Gun Laws

We'll be talking about gun laws as time goes by.

—DONALD TRUMP

AS TIME GOES BY.

There will be time, of course, to have this discussion. "Not now" is not the same as never.

It must be on a day when there has been no recent gun violence. So not today, and not tomorrow, and not the day after that. But someday. There is no Catch-22 here, where because there are not sensible gun laws, it is always too soon after a major gun tragedy to talk about sensible gun laws. No.

There is a perfect moment that exists for such a conversation, just after the moment of silence and just before life resumes. If you slice time thinly enough you will find it, like plucking an atom of gold from the air. It lasts only a millisecond, but it is the right time, and words spoken then will not fall on deaf ears. (The discussion must be brief. Just a second too late and it will be the wrong time again.) But it is possible.

When the time arrives, we must come to the issue without politics. (Politics have seeped into our chicken and our Pepsi, and our late-night talk show hosts give addresses after tragedies that ought to come from the president. Politics is football and wishing people a happy holiday and ordering a coffee.) We must avoid politics. We must approach it with a perfectly blank slate, as blank and void as Megyn Kelly's new NBC show.

There will be a day, and we will know. It will be when there is a president in power whom everyone likes and respects. When Congress is no longer beholden to the National Rifle Association for ever-more-baffling sums. When we have ended gerrymandering and taken action on climate change. After we amend the electoral college. Right after the last of the Confederate statues comes down, maybe a week or two after we have fixed sexism. It will be three or four days after we look around and notice we are living in a truly postracial society. The day after your Beanie Baby collection finally accrues its full expected value. One brisk afternoon, you will get into an argument on the Internet, and it will make you change your mind about something and feel better about humanity. And then you will know: Today is the day for the conversation about gun laws.

It will be before the sun burns out and all human life is extinct, probably.

So we must wait at least until then, to avoid politicizing the issue. That is only reasonable and fair. That is quite a different thing from "never."

October 3, 2017

I Am Sick of These Children Demanding Safe Spaces

The left's propaganda shaped a new generation of young adults, who then parroted all that malarkey about the "patriarchy" and then they came up with their own new phrases like "microaggressions" and "safe spaces" and "white privilege."

—LAURA INGRAHAM, AFTER COMING UNDER
FIRE FOR MAKING FUN OF A PARKLAND
SHOOTING SURVIVOR

I AM SICK OF THESE children and their demands for safe spaces.

Safe spaces! Back in my day, all we had were dangerous spaces. People would call you names that would turn your ears blue. Everyone had measles, mumps, and rubella, just as a matter of course, and we did not go crawling to our family physicians for so-called vaccines. Disease was a ritual of childhood. We toughed it out. We built character.

We did not have satellite radio or the Internet. We had to make our own electricity by rubbing sticks together. Everyone had six guns apiece, which we used to fight world wars. (There has not been a good world war for too long, and kids have gotten needlessly soft.) When children misbehaved, their parents were strongly encouraged to hit them with a rod.

Nobody wore safety belts. The water was full of mercury. The fish were full of sewage. Nobody recycled ANYTHING. When someone fell ill, you just hoped and prayed. (More things should be resolved that way: not with regulations or attempts at solutions but by wishing and hoping and thinking and praying. That was good enough for us, and any change in the world since then has been a change for the worse.)

We used to crawl to school uphill both ways in blinding snow-storms. We used to drink water from lead pipes. Some children still do this, but not nearly enough of them. There was smog in the air as thick as a man's fist. You could smoke on airplanes. In fact, you were encouraged to do so. It was this pointless suffering that made me who I am.

Dare I deny these benefits to the children of today?

I look at kids these days and I despair. They need to man up and solve their own problems. They need to stop demanding to be coddled. Children now are wimps, and far too few of them have experienced the grit developed by being exposed to communicable diseases, or urged to ride bicycles without helmets.

Now, suddenly, they want to get rid of guns, too. The one thing I know is that we cannot stop guns. There is no point in discussing that; that is an immutable aspect of human nature. Children need to toughen up and learn how to care for themselves. They should learn CPR. And they need to stop using rude words when they respond to me, specifically, although I get to use those words back, as it will make them stronger and hardier.

If we let these kids have their way, soon there will not be danger anywhere. They will be able to go to school in the morning and feel confident that they will be able to come home in the evening. This is a radical thing to ask. I remember no such certainty. It is, therefore, undesirable. These children are weak. I do not want my children to live in a better world than the world that I grew up in, or the one we live in now. That would be to admit that things have progressed, and I do not admit that.

That is what conservatism means to me: the ability to pass the dangers and privations of my life on to the generation that will come after. The hope that their lives will be, if not actively worse than mine, then certainly no better. The idea that I suffered not because there were no better choices but because the suffering was inherently good.

If anyone were to think differently, that would be the real tragedy. Children are weak. They are whiners. They deserve my mockery.

If I were forced to spend a single day in which I did not insult youth, that would be the real tragedy. If I had to let any argument I disagreed with go unanswered, because attacking a child would be ghoulish—that would be letting them win.

I am sick of these children and their demands for safe spaces. Safe spaces! I refuse to modify my argument in any way to reflect the fact that what they are asking to be kept safe from is not words but bullets. I refuse to be silent even for a moment.

When I was young, children were seen but not heard. If children suddenly started to be heard, that would be the greatest tragedy of all.

March 29, 2018

This Magic Is
Too Strong to Stop

IT DOES NOT MATTER WHAT it was to begin with. A wallet. A pipe. A cellphone. It makes no difference. The phenomenon remains the same every time.

In the morning, it is very clearly a cellphone. Anyone who looks at it can see it.

In the afternoon, it is still very clearly a cellphone. It sends texts. It makes calls. Its screen lights up.

But in the evening, the transformation occurs. A police officer sees the cellphone, sees that the hand holding it belongs to a black man, and suddenly, quite without warning, it becomes a gun.

This keeps happening.

Suppose we close all the gun shows. Suppose we close all the loopholes. Suppose we take guns off the shelves at sporting goods stores. It will not matter, because of this mysterious phenomenon (observed mostly by police officers in the moments before an "officer-involved shooting") where a completely innocuous object becomes, for a moment or two, a gun. It can even be a child who picks it up.

It cannot be that police officers do not know what guns look like. They seem perfectly capable of wielding them themselves. It is not that they do not know what cellphones look like. It can only be magic, and the magic does not change.

On April 4, it was a metal pipe. The man who held it was named Saheed Vassell. He was the father of a teenage son. It scarcely took twenty-seven seconds for officers to see the pipe transform into a gun. By the time he was dead, it had already changed back.

Later, when officers are called on to justify their actions in these deaths, what matters is not whether their fear was reasonable, but whether the fear was real. And what is more frightening than impossible sorcery? Fear brings a magic all its own, by which cellphones become guns and people "bulk up" to run through bullets. It transforms teenagers into Hulk Hogan, into demons. You cannot say for certain what object will mutate next. It could be a Bible. It could be a hand in a pocket. With a fear so immense, you are right to act no matter how harmless the target may seem—whether it is a cellphone, or a pipe, or a father, or a child.

That is what makes these deaths justified: that moment of fear, that transforms something ordinary—a father, an iPhone— and makes it deadly. If these things could not be, if there were no fearful magic involved, these deaths would be utterly senseless.

No, it certainly cannot be that it is not happening at all.

So it is clear we can never solve the gun epidemic in this country. It is not because we cannot pass the laws. It is because there is sorcery happening, and until we stop this sorcery, there can be no progress.

April 5, 2018

How to Sleep at Night When Families Are Being Separated at the Border

THE TRICK IS FORGETTING THAT they are children.

If you remember that they are children, you will not be able to go on with any of this. If you remember when you were a child, and frightened, and everything seemed impossibly big and loud and sharp and hard except a certain pair of familiar arms, this will have to stop.

The trick is forgetting that there is such a word as "child." To remember words like "bad hombre" and "thug" instead. You do not have to say "animals," if you do not want to. There are other ways. "To assume that just because of someone's age or gender or whatever that they don't pose a threat would be wrong," Sean Spicer bumbled last year.

"Deterrent" is a good word, too. "Zero-tolerance" is even better. And no one likes the idea of a "human shield."

The trick is to wrap this up in words so tightly that you cannot see the child inside.

The trick is to reassure yourself that this is what they deserve, that what makes you different, that what makes your children children and not threats or thugs is something within your control. That the fact that you have nothing to run from is because of your particular virtue. ("You're a parent. Don't you have any empathy? Come on, Sarah, you're a parent!" Brian Karem tried during the White House press briefing last Thursday. "Brian, God, settle down.... I know you want to get some more TV time, but that's not what this is about.")

The trick is to remind yourself that this could be worse. That some of them are, of course, not in cages. (This is a fact of which Breitbart.com is quite proud. They are not *all* in cages.) When they are literally torn from their mothers' breasts, which you thought happened only in the careless metaphors of people losing online arguments, they are not also smeared with soot like Dickensian orphans and given coarse rags to wear, at least not on the footage released to media. They are orphans, sure, but there is nothing *Dickensian* about them.

The trick is not to admit that this is happening. The trick is not to see pictures of it, except the footage the Department of Health and Human Services provides that barely shows any children at all, mostly long shots of murals (a poster of the Justice League; a lingering shot of a seasick-looking Superman, smiling miserably down from a wall) with the occasional glimpse of children that does not show any of the running and screaming and attempting suicide.

None of this requires magic that has never been performed before. We were adept at it for centuries. If we squinted just right, it was possible to look and see not a child but a commodity ("For Sale ... A Girl, Eleven years old, used to the care of children. A Boy, Ten years old"), or a threat that needed to be locked behind barbed wire ("The whole Japanese population is properly under suspicion as to its loyalties.... [T]hey need to be restrained for the safety of California and the United States").

We are still adept at it when it is convenient. When the alternative would be to admit that we have put a bullet into a child, it is amazing how the child transforms into a man and the toy in his hand mutates into a dangerous weapon. It is only true that we have never done this, that this is not what we do, if you forget that they were children, too, before.

But these *are* children, now, and they have not been here very long, and they are still learning where everything is. And they are still at an age where something can be unthinkable because there has simply not been enough time to think it yet, where a thing that has only happened for a year can be a thing that has happened *for as long as you can remember.*

Time is different when you are a child. Every day stretches into forever. New worlds can be invented and discarded in the course of a single afternoon. And America can be a place that has always done a thing or America can be a place that has never done a thing except in stories or in nightmares.

If we stop this now, right now, this instant, after a year or two or three there will be children who know that America would never do such a thing. And then we must keep not doing it. We must stop this until they are not children any longer, and then never do it again.

The trick is not forgetting they are children. The trick is never forgetting again.

June 18, 2018

Play the "Woman Card" and Reap These Rewards

Frankly, if Hillary Clinton were a man, I don't think she'd get 5 percent of the vote. The only thing she's got going is the woman's card.

—TRUMP, AFTER WINNING FIVE PRIMARIES

AH YES, THE WOMAN CARD.

I have been carrying one of these for years, proudly.

It is great. It entitles you to a sizable discount on your earnings everywhere you go (average 21 percent, but can be anywhere from 9 percent to 37 percent, depending on what study you're reading and what edition of the Woman Card you have). If you shop with the Woman Card at the grocery, you will get to pay 11 percent more for all the same products as men, but now they are pink.

It's about more than discounts, though.

Hook up the Woman Card to your TV and you will get a barrage of commercials telling you that you did something wrong with your face and must buy ointment immediately so as not to become a Hideous Crone. Also, you are now expected to spend your whole life removing hair from your body, except for the areas of your body where your hair must be long and luxurious. (Do not get these two areas confused!)

The great news is that if you use your Woman Card to hurt other women, you get access to a special place in hell.

Take the Woman Card on the subway with you, put your headphones in, and you are guaranteed a free, lengthy, one-on-one conversation or lecture from a man who will not leave you alone unless you also remembered to bring your I Have a Boyfriend Card (they accept no substitutes).

Show the Woman Card to your health-care provider and you will enjoy new limits on your reproductive rights, depending on what the legislators of your state have decided is wise. Get ready to have a lot of things about your body explained to you!

The Woman Card is not, itself, a form of birth control (no matter what Todd Akin suggests) but it can prevent you from getting coverage for yours.

Use the Woman Card at the library to get a book with squiggly pastel handwriting on the cover that Gay Talese will not take seriously.

Present the Woman Card to a man you have just met at a party and it is good for one detailed, patronizing explanation of the subject you literally got your PhD in.

Offer it to someone on the red carpet and, instead of any substantive questions about your work, you will get a barrage of inquiries EXCLUSIVELY about what you are wearing.

On the bright side, running for office as a Woman Cardholder is a blast, because it allows people to accuse your female supporters of only liking you because of your gender. Don't try suggesting the opposite! That doesn't work.

Show off the Woman Card on your way to work and you will get free comments from total strangers, telling you to smile. Play it in the sciences and you will get to leave the sciences.

Take the Woman Card anywhere and you will instantly be

surrounded by men who feel entitled to your time. Also, to your space. Do not take up too much space; the Woman Card does not cover that. It also does not cover female protagonists or not being harassed online. You are on your own for those. The Woman Card doesn't even entitle you to shorter lines in the restroom. Frankly, as fun as it is to be a member of the exclusive club, and as much as I enjoy the occasional door-holding, I'm not even sure I want to re-up this year.

But it's not all fun discounts and free experiences!

The Woman Card entitles you to constant scrutiny and judgment from all corners at all times, whether you asked for it or not. Try talking! Or rather, don't.

You can also use it in fun card games, including but not limited to Go Fish (what your boss says when you ask for a raise), Can You Have It All? (fundamentally identical to War but you can't win), Sorry! (compete to see who can say this the most in the course of a single meeting), Don't Wake Daddy (mom has to do all the child-rearing by default), and Five-Card Slut Poker (for men, this is called Five-Card Stud, but this is the double-standard edition).

Unlike Man Cards, Woman Cards do not increase in value as they age. In fact, they depreciate. Do not collect Woman Cards. Even in mint condition, they are worthless.

April 27, 2016

That Five-Year-Old Refugee Has Diabolical Plans

That's why we slow it down and make sure that if they are a five year old that maybe they're with their parents and they don't pose a threat. . . . To assume that just because of someone's age or gender or whatever that they don't pose a threat would be wrong.

—PRESS SECRETARY SEAN SPICER, WHEN ASKED ABOUT THE FIVE-YEAR-OLD IRANIAN BOY WHO WAS DETAINED UNDER PRESIDENT TRUMP'S EXECUTIVE ORDER ON REFUGEES

SEAN SPICER IS QUITE RIGHT to be concerned. This five-year-old boy waiting at the airport certainly has a diabolical plan. All five-year-old children do.

When the five-year-old comes to this country, he will begin his hostile takeover almost immediately. He is going to touch everything in the house and his hands will be sticky for some undefinable reason and nothing in the house will ever feel entirely not sticky ever again.

He will sow disinformation. He will run up and down the aisle of the airplane creating chaos and making fake plane noises with his mouth, even though he is clearly not a plane. He will say the floor is lava. He will say he is a dinosaur. He will say he is Batman. He will say he is a doctor who can vaccinate you against cooties. All of these will be lies.

He will commit sabotage. He will knock down his block towers with a thunderous crash when you are on the telephone. He will spill his Legos on the carpet for you to walk across barefoot in the middle of the night and make you blaspheme God.

But he will not stop there. He will tell interminable stories. He will draw horrible propaganda art where your head is too big and both your arms are sticks and your mouth is a horrible pool full of yellow boulder teeth.

He has plans to turn his bed into a spaceship without registering first with NASA. He has plans to invite friends over from school and hold them hostage behind the couch with his whole army of stuffed hippos.

He has plans to carry his sinister associate Bear Bear with him everywhere, to bed and to the dinner table, and even to school, and we know how Betsy DeVos feels about bears in schools. Besides, Bear Bear is a foreign operative with a missing eye and almost none of his original fur, always silent, and his motives cannot be adequately discerned.

He has plans to let go of your hand and run off giggling because he thinks the world is all like him on the inside and there is no one who does not understand that he means no harm—how could they?—and he wants to play.

Oh yes, the five-year-old boy has diabolical plans. Look at him, standing in the airport. He is not even four feet high, but his mind is whirling with plans: to go to a strange new school and learn a strange new language and make strange new friends and teach them to draw all over the walls with crayon. And at recess, he may not share. He has plans to sit up past bedtime in a house where the sound of bombs falling does not keep him awake. He has plans to commit awful acts of sabotage like flushing strange things down the toilet, because here there is a toilet to flush. He has plans to grow up to become the most terrifying thing in the world: an American.

And if you turn him away—you will be very lucky if he does not have other plans.

January 30, 2017

I Will Not Take My Husband's Name

I WILL NOT TAKE my husband's name. He uses it for work. It would be cruel to leave him without a name, simply because we have told the world that we are in love.

It would be sad to see him drift listlessly through cocktail parties with an empty name tag. "I'm Dave," someone would say to him, "I work in synergies," and he would pause, and blink, and have no answer. His business cards would be a job description and a void of white space. He would, I suppose, save money on monogrammed towels, as every towel would be, for him, a monogrammed towel, but equally no towel would be a monogrammed towel.

Suppose we were to become separated in a crowd. If I had taken his name, I would have nothing to call. I would have to stand in the middle of the crowd and scream and scream, and perhaps he would not even turn his head. To take his name would be, for calling purposes, functionally to transform him into a cat.

I will not take his name. I think it looks good on him. I am used to it. This precise arrangement of letters and syllables suits him, and without it, how would I send him emails?

I will take neither his last name nor his first name. I contemplated perhaps the last name. He could get by without one, after all. Cher does. So does Bruce (in Jersey, anyway), although it might be difficult on credit cards.

I will not take my husband's name. It would make him impossible to enter as a contact in my phone; ten digits with no words attached.

I will not take my husband's name. How could we sing "Happy Birthday" to him? To start and then fall silent at the climax would depress the other patrons in restaurants.

I will not take my husband's name. Nor will I take his face nor his reflection nor his shadow (though I did consider, for a moment, taking his shadow). And I will not take his voice; I have no shell in which to store it.

Even if he does not use his name, it belongs to him.

I will not take my husband's name. I will be merciful.

June 25, 2018

Part V

HOW NOT TO DO THINGS WRONG

THERE IS NOTHING MORE EMBARRASSING than to do things wrong! What words are good to say, and what words are bad to say? Which tiny fork should you use to eat salad, which tiny fork is for dessert, and which tiny fork bears a hideous curse and should be destroyed immediately if it is ever placed in front of you? Society is full of these questions! There are many written rules, like, murder is bad—but equally there are unwritten rules, like, if you are responsible for enough murder, far enough away, and wear a nice suit, people still have to be polite to you at cocktail parties. Here is how to say and do things correctly in this wonderful world, with some beautiful guidelines for your speech to be more perfect, and some examples of how to write well and correctly about the news that is going on. You will soon be getting the hang of it! Look no further to be Good and Accurate!

Famous Quotes, the Way a Woman Ought to Say Them in a Meeting

I HAVE TAKEN THE LIBERTY of translating some famous sentences into the way a woman would have to phrase them during a meeting to avoid being perceived as angry, threatening, or (gasp!) bitchy. Start with your thought. Then say it as though you were offering a groveling apology for an unspecified error. This will prevent embarrassing mistakes!

"Give me liberty, or give me death."
Woman in a Meeting: "Dave, if I could, I could just—I just really feel like if we had liberty it would be terrific, and the alternative would just be awful, you know? That's just how it strikes me. I don't know."

"I have a dream today!"
Woman in a Meeting: "I'm sorry, I just had this idea—it's probably crazy, but—look, just as long as we're throwing things out here—I had sort of an idea or vision about maybe the future?"

"Mr. Gorbachev, tear down this wall!"

Woman in a Meeting: "I'm sorry, Mikhail, if I could? Didn't mean to cut you off there. Can we agree that this wall maybe isn't quite doing what it should be doing? Just looking at everything everyone's been saying, it seems like we could consider removing it. Possibly. I don't know, what does the room feel?"

"The only thing we have to fear is fear itself."

Woman in a Meeting: "I have to say—I'm sorry—I have to say this. I don't think we should be as scared of non-fear things as maybe we are? If that makes sense? Sorry, I feel like I'm rambling."

"Ask not what your country can do for you. Ask what you can do for your country."

Woman in a Meeting: "I'm not an expert, Dave, but I feel like maybe you could accomplish more by maybe shifting your focus from asking things from the government and instead looking at things that we can all do ourselves? Just a thought. Just a thought. Take it for what it's worth."

"Let my people go."

Woman in a Meeting: "Pharaoh, listen, I totally hear where you're coming from on this. I totally do. And I don't want to butt in if you've come to a decision here, but, just, I have to say, would you consider that an argument for maybe releasing these people could conceivably have merit? Or is that already off the table?"

"I came. I saw. I conquered."

Woman in a Meeting: "I don't want to toot my own horn here at all but I definitely have been to those places and was just honored to be a part of it as our team did such a wonderful job of conquering them."

"We hold these truths to be self-evident, that all men are created equal."
Woman in a Meeting: "I'm sorry, it really feels to me like we're all equal, you know? I just feel really strongly on this."

"I have not yet begun to fight."
Woman in a Meeting: "Dave, I'm not going to fight you on this."

"I will be heard."
Woman in a Meeting: "Sorry to interrupt. No, go on, Dave. Finish what you had to say."

October 13, 2015

Some
Interpersonal Verbs,
Conjugated by Gender

THE SAMPLE SENTENCES BELOW demonstrate the proper English usage of interpersonal verbs, inflected for mood, tense, and gender.

UNIT 1

He is drinking; he is drunk; he was drunk.

He is just seventeen; he was just seventeen.

Remember that he is just a kid; remember that he was just a kid; you must remember he was just a kid.

He cannot know what he is doing; he could not know what he was doing; he cannot have known what he was doing.

See your way clear to letting this go; you must see your way clear to letting this go.

He has his future ahead of him; he had his future ahead of him.

This will ruin his life; this is going to ruin his life.

He makes a mistake; he made a mistake; people make mistakes; mistakes were made.

He did something; she had something done to her; something happened.

These things happen.

She is drinking; she is drunk; she was drunk.

She is fifteen; she was fifteen.

She is putting herself in this position; she put herself in that position.

She should know better; she should have known better.

She must think about his future; she must think about her future.

She must say nothing; she will say nothing; she says nothing; she said nothing.

What happens here will stay here; what happens here stays here; what happens here stays.

She carries this; she will carry this.

An incident occurred; an incident derailed her life; her life was derailed.

These things happen.

She should not say anything; she will ruin his life; it will not be real unless she says something.

She should not have waited so long to speak; she should have said something; it could not have been real if she did not say anything.

These allegations will ruin his life; making these allegations will ruin someone's life; she will ruin her life making these allegations.

She went on to lead a productive life, so how bad can it have been?

She did not go on to lead a productive life, so how can we trust what she has to say?

If it is true, why would she want to remain anonymous? Now that we know her name, we are coming to her house.

It happens. It happened. It was a long time ago.

She waits. She says nothing.

She should not have waited. She should not have said nothing.

She remembers it happened. She remembers it happened to her. She remembers he did something.

She says something.

How can she remember? Does she remember? Is it possible to remember? I don't remember—who can remember?

She wore something. Did she wear something? What did she wear?

Did she drink? Was she drinking?

Did he drink? Was he drinking?

She should have been responsible. He cannot have been responsible.

It is very hard to imagine that anything happened. Did it happen? It was a long time ago. She said nothing.

He does not remember.

He remembers that it did not happen. He remembers that he did nothing. He remembers that he was absent.

UNIT 2 (ADVANCED)

If it happened (although it did not happen), it would not have been wrong.

If it happened (it may have happened; he did not do it, but it may have happened), it was only to be expected.

These things happen. (He did not do it.)

These things happen. (Even if he did it, it was only a thing that sometimes happens.)

We cannot know what happened; she does not know what happened; he knows what happened.

Nothing happens; nothing happened; something happened to her; he did nothing; this is how it always happens.

This is how a thing he did became something that happened to her; this is how something he did becomes something that happens.

This is how this keeps happening.

September 19, 2018

How to Fact-Check

ONE OF THE IMPORTANT FUNCTIONS of journalism is to check facts. Sometimes people make statements that sound true, but in fact are not—and vice versa! The role of the fact-checker—like us, here at FactFind—is to make certain we can tell which is which! Here are a few examples of tricky sentences to fact-check.

The Age of Man Is Over. The Time of the Orc Has Come!

Rating: two truthcicles of a possible five!

It's very difficult to quantify when an "age" begins and ends. In geologic time, ages last for millions of years, whereas Man has only been here on Middle-earth for a small fraction of that. To say that the Age of Man is over, Man would have to have existed for a long enough period to impact Middle-earth, already a dubious proposition, if you consult any trained geologist. As to the second claim, it is certainly true that Orcs are more numerous now than they have ever been—and the new race of Uruk-hai is making enormous strides! So although nobody has been alive for an Age, it is possible to say with some accuracy that the Orc is having a moment. A full age? Maybe not. Still, this isn't entirely a false premise. And if men keep faring as badly as they did at Helm's Deep, they may not be long for this world! By the way, who said this? Was there any more context?

All Newsmen and Immigrants Deserve to Be Burned at the Stake

Rating: three untruth-slices of a possible four!

It's extremely difficult to state with certainty what anyone deserves, let alone a large, heterogeneous group of people like journalists and immigrants. To do this, you would need a lot of data, much more data than we at FactFind currently possess! Technically, we are journalists, and I sure wouldn't like to be burned at the stake, whether I deserve to be, or not. The question of what people deserve has been contemplated since the dawn of time by philosophers and jurists, and nobody has been able to come up with a clear answer. But one thing we can do is look at the law, which has not recommended burning anyone at the stake for a crime for more than six hundred years! That's a pretty clear precedent—it would suggest that, in our jurisprudential tradition, *nobody* deserves to be burned at the stake. This being said, every group of people, like every standard barrel of apples, contains some bad apples. (Source: Apple Barrel Comparison, 2014). So is it possible to say that ALL newsmen and immigrants DON'T deserve to be burned at stakes? Well, just to be safe, let's give this three out of four.

Sometimes People Make Statements in Bad Faith That Don't Deserve to Be Evaluated as Fact

We give this statement 50 percent. That feels even-handed, right?

How to Speak Woman

I HAVE READ ALL THE critiques of women's vocal mannerisms and tics. I have come to a few simple conclusions, which I have distilled into the following thirteen tips.

1. Never speak in run-on sentences. Use only sentences that Hemingway would use. Speak curtly. Speak of fish and fighting, and the deep wisdom no woman can know. Speak of hills and strong liquor. Speak of Scott Fitzgerald and his fatal weakness.
2. Never let the word "just" pass your lips. If you find that you have used the word "just" even once, smite mightily about yourself with a mace, lest anyone live to tell the tale and lose you the respect of your colleagues.
3. Never end sentences with a question mark, even when you are asking a question. This may baffle and alarm everyone around you, but better that than the alternative.
4. In fact, avoid questions entirely, lest someone hear you speaking with a rising inflection and take away your place in the workforce. When you wish to ask a question, have a man ask it for you, to save face.
5. *Never* speak with a rising inflection. If you must speak with any inflection at all, speak with a falling inflection.
6. Do not use baby talk, not even to babies. Especially not to babies. Avoid speaking to babies in general, as they do not control the workforce and cannot offer you advancement.

7. Never apologize. Not even once. Not for yourself, and certainly not for America. Never let "sorry" leave your lips. If you wish to play the board game of that name, point at it and growl.

8. Never creak. You should sooner croak than creak.

9. When you form words at all, which should be but rarely, make certain they come out in a low, gravelly growl, like a hungover Joe Cocker who has just gargled shards of glass. Strive to sound like a cigarette would sound if it could talk. Strive to rumble like thunder that has taken a class to counteract its vocal fry. If you sound like the love child of Darth Vader and a female Ent, you have achieved your purpose. Speak so that those who hear you wonder aloud and say, "Surely this speaker is a man. Or a grizzly bear who has swallowed a man whole."

10. Most of the time, make no sound at all. Let your actions speak for you. Speak with your fists, never your hands.

11. In general, communicate only by tearing off the arms of those with whom you are displeased. Wave these arms like flags, in a kind of gruff semaphore. To express feelings, roll rocks downhill with rude emoji carved on them.

12. Remember, be confident. You are woman. Hear you roar. It is the only vocalization you can freely make lest you be hounded off the airwaves and out of the workforce.

13. GRRRRR ARRRG. GRRRRRR. RRRRR.

July 28, 2015

How to Parent Wrong

THERE ARE SO MANY PARENTING fads, it is hard to keep them straight!

Here are your options.

Helicopter Parenting: You hover frantically over your child at all times, shredding pigeons in your rotating blades.

Free-Range Parenting: Your children eat grass and roam at will so that their flesh will become more tender and juicy than that of their cage-bred counterparts.

Lawnmower/Snowplow Parenting: You knock all obstacles out of your child's path like a—bulldozer? Why didn't they go with bulldozer when naming this parenting style? Lawnmowers and snowplows aren't the same thing at all! Make sure you're doing the one that is right for your climate.

Juggernaut Parenting: You knock all obstacles out of your child's path while shouting "I'M THE JUGGERNAUT!"

Tiger Parenting: You are maniacally devoted to your child's excellence in all things and will fight your child tooth and nail until that child gets into Princeton.

Free-Range Tiger Parenting: Your children can roam at will, but must drag pianos with them to practice.

Free-Range Helicopter Parenting: Your children can roam at will, but you hover overhead in a helicopter.

Free-Range Attachment Parenting: Your children can wander anywhere at will, and you just happen to be there too.

Tiger Attachment Parenting: To help with discipline, your child is attached to a live tiger.

Helicopter Tiger Parenting: OH GOD, WHO'S PILOTING THAT THING? It's a BIG CAT!

Ironic Hipster Parenting: You're screwing up your child on purpose.

Locavore Parenting: You only eat local children.

Trump Parenting: "I'm the best parent, the greatest, and your childhood is going to be huge!" you tell your child, repeatedly, for eighteen years, offering no other guidance.

Parenting 90X: This parenting technique looks a lot more doable when the guy in the video does it.

Outsource Helicopter Parenting: You hire someone else to micromanage your children's lives.

Lawnmower Attachment Parenting: You chew up life before feeding it to your child.

French Parenting: Where are my children? Give me wine.

Dickens Parenting: Children are orphans.

Disney Parenting: One parent is mysteriously deceased but the other one is voiced by James Earl Jones.

Lion Parenting: Everything the light touches is yours, you tell your child, before being stampeded to death by wildebeests.

Backseat Parenting: You let the child make all his own decisions, then second-guess them.

Joan Crawford Parenting: All your parenting decisions are bad, but your child is at least getting a good memoir out of it.

Sondheim Parenting: Sing out, Louise!

Sims Parenting: Child sometimes plays chess for three days straight, but equally also sometimes plays video games for three days straight. No one wants to talk about pirates with him. Oh no, the pool ladder's gone!

Paleo Parenting: You abandon your child on a rock outcropping to fend for himself.

SoulCycle Parenting: You leave your child at home to go to SoulCycle.

Traditional Parenting: You have six children and all of them perish before age four. You are a serf.

Bible-Based Parenting: You have eleven sons. Ten of them sell the eleventh into slavery because they are angry about his fashion choices.

Sitcom Parenting: Oh, Dad!

Philosophical Parenting: Because I said so, that's why.

Princeton Mom Parenting: "WHY AREN'T YOU MARRIED YET? YOUR YOUTH IS SLIPPING AWAY!" you shout, as your daughter emerges from the womb.

Dada Parenting: You find someone else's child and write R. Mutt on him.

Surrealist Parenting: Your child is a lobster.

Kafka Parenting: When your child won't come out of his room, you assume that it is because he has transformed into a monstrous vermin.

MOMA Parenting: Your child is not a child but an art installation! You are Tilda Swinton.

Sharknado Parenting: Your parenting is so bad it's good.

Objectivist Parenting: You do not live for your children, nor do you ask your children to live for you. Stop crying, Little Roark, and let enlightened self-interest guide you.

Just remember, at the end of the day, there's only one way to parent: wrong.

September 3, 2015

What to Call Racist Remarks Instead of Calling Them Racist Remarks

SO, SOMEONE HAS SAID SOMETHING RACIST. But you don't want to *SAY* they have said something racist. That would be upsetting! What do you do? For anyone still struggling on this point, here are some further euphemisms for "racist" to add pizzazz to your headlines! Don't worry, everyone will know what you mean.

+ Racially tinged
+ Very fine remarks
+ Heritage-loving remarks
+ Remarks that seem anxious about the economy
+ Remarks that would be upset if you called them racist
+ Remarks that some people still think would make a good Halloween costume
+ Remarks that march to their own drummer against the tide of political correctness
+ Remarks that would still be acceptable as a logo of a major sports franchise
+ Remarks that, if Disney had made them into a movie, would have been put into a vault and sealed forever

from public view except that they are hinted at on certain theme-park rides

+ Racially cloudy remarks with a hint of controversy meatballs

+ Remarks that if they were a soup, George Wallace would eat that soup and go "mmmmmm I love it," but we can't specify why

+ Polarizing remarks, in the sense that if they were a magnet, the things that would be stuck on one end of the magnet would be racists although it might be a coincidence, who can say!

+ Maybe these remarks were born with it, maybe it was racism, don't make us pick!

+ Remarks that, if they were printed on a T-shirt, *might* sell well at Trump rallies, hypothetically

+ Forgotten American remarks

+ Remarks we would do well to listen to before the next election

+ Remarks capable of summoning dogs from many miles away, and when surveyed you discover that all the dogs are racist but who can say there was any correlation

+ Remarks that Starbucks will need to have a Conversation about

+ Remarks not out of place coming from the mouth of the president of the United States

May 29, 2018

So, You Must Speak to the Woman Who Is Wearing Headphones

"How to Talk to a Woman Who Is Wearing Headphones" is advice that exists, thanks to something called TheMod-ernMan.com. But it does not go far enough! Anyone who wishes to attempt this must be fully prepared.

SO IT HAS COME TO THIS.

You must speak to the woman who is wearing headphones.

I am so, so sorry.

You must pray that she is single and looking and will wish to hear your words.

It is not enough for her to be single.

She must also be looking, or there is no hope for you.

But you already know this.

You have seen what happened to the other men who tried to speak.

The whole Panera is littered with what remains of the men who came before you.

They tried to speak to the Woman Who Is Wearing Headphones.

They failed.

Remember the training and you may yet survive.

Remember what they told you.

You must be confident, relaxed, and easygoing.

You must show no fear.

If you show fear, she will strike.

Speak calmly, they said.

Show confidence.

Do not blink.

If you blink, she will know.

If you blink, she will move much closer, so close that you can hear the whisper of what is in her headphones.

That is much too close.

You have no choice.

These are your instructions.

You can talk to anyone, you tell yourself.

It is only a woman, you tell yourself.

But you know that it is not.

Women were something different.

Your comrade made the awful mistake of talking to the Woman Who Is Reading a Book on the Subway. You watched it happen.

He made her look up from the book and her basilisk eyes fell on him, unblinking, and he melted.

You still remember the screams.

They were so horrible that the city lay awake for days trying to forget them.

You do not know how it happened.

But the women who stood there politely and were receptacles for your words are gone.

They once smiled politely and they laughed even and sometimes they would make a spark with you.

But something changed in the air or perhaps the water and the women do not stand there and listen any longer.

The city is full of men who have been turned to stone.

You opened the door to your neighbor's apartment and there was a startled deer standing inside wearing a college sweatshirt. You think it used to be your neighbor but you are not certain.

You have changed your route to work so that you do not have to pass the stone men with their open, screaming mouths.

Yesterday half your comrades were ordered to shout "Smile!" at the Woman Who Is Walking.

And the woman did. Too wide.

So wide that her mouth engulfed the street and became a vast cavern.

Six of your friends were devoured.

You could hear the unladylike slurping sounds from blocks away as you beat a hasty retreat between the Scylla of the Woman Who Has Put Her Bag Next to Her on a Bar Stool and the Charybdis of the Woman Who Is Just Jogging.

You did not attempt to speak to either of them.

They passed you.

You were left unscathed.

But that was before they came to your apartment and gave you the orders.

So here you are.

It has come to this.

You are about to talk to the Woman in Headphones.

My God, I pity you.

You are close now. Almost in range.

Before the Woman and behind her the ground is littered with shoes and hats and pick-up manuals and AXE body spray.

She sits patiently gnawing on a thigh bone.

You do not think she is single or looking.

You cannot make out the words she is listening to.

You know how this will go.

You know what the headphones mean.

You know what will happen when you ask her to remove the headphones.

August 30, 2016

Part VI

FINALLY, WE HEAR FROM MEN, MEASLES, AND A PIGEON

OH NO! I HAVE MADE A HUGE MISTAKE! I HAVE not exposed you to a sufficient diversity of viewpoints, which has been quite naughty of me! Indeed, I have been doing the unthinkable all this time, for this whole book. I have not let you hear from Men! I have, but I have not done so exclusively, which is also a very bad form of oppression. Although it is always unfair to speak broadly of an entire set of people, I do not think it is inaccurate to assert that Gentlemen have a Lot to Say, and that all of it is Good and Worth Hearing! If a Gentleman is even briefly asked to hold his peace, it is a country-ruining mistake, up with which we must not put. Oh, forgive me! Forgive me! Please, feast your eyes on all of these wise things, a broad range of remarks from the very finest male minds, a wide diversity of opinions from many wise and temperate men, and also a pigeon and a measles germ!

Please Stop Vaccinating Your Children. I Want to Go to Disneyland.

ARE YOU THINKING OF VACCINATING YOUR KIDS?

I wish you wouldn't.

I know what you're going to say. "You're a measles germ. You're biased."

But maybe you're the one who's biased. Ever thought about that?

I see your charts. I hear you calling the resurgence of measles "devastating." That's hurtful.

"There's more measles now," you say. "That is a bad thing." Maybe it's a bad thing. Or maybe it's a GREAT thing. Maybe a beautiful specimen that was hunted almost to extinction is making a surprise comeback, and you should be a little more supportive!

I mean, when someone hunts down all the spotted owls you're like "Oh, boo hoo, we're wiping out a species, waaah, conservation, blaaah"—but suddenly it's okay to destroy measles and its whole microbial culture and you're all congratulating yourselves? Do you see the inconsistency here? Come on.

I think there are two sides to this issue, and it is important that we hear both of them out.

After all, you've heard Jenny McCarthy on this issue, and she is definitely a human person, not a large number of measles viruses cleverly disguised as a human person by standing on each other's porous membranes under a big coat. The idea that she is not a human person is completely ridiculous. It is just another lie spread by scientists, like the idea that having measles is somehow "bad" or "lesser" than *not* having measles. But just so we're clear: Jenny is definitely one of you. Would talented human actor Donnie Wahlberg kiss a bunch of measles viruses? I rest my case.

"You should be exterminated," you are saying. You know who else said that? Don't make me say it. He had a mustache.

I know there are scientists saying things like "YOU NEED TO GET VACCINATED."

I'm like, "Whoa, scientists! Cool your jets!" I think we can all agree this is no time for panic. Maybe vaccination is completely safe and keeps you from catching diseases and maybe there are lots of facts that support that, but maybe we're all putting too much emphasis on facts and not enough emphasis on Anecdotal Feelings That Some Parents Told This One Doctor About.

In that same article, doctors call people who don't get vaccines "stupid." That sounds like bullying to me. These "doctors" sound less like medical professionals and more like MEANIES. And I don't listen to MEANIES. Do you?

Sure, the connection between autism and vaccines has been disproved by science, but you know what else has been disproved by science? Dragons. And who wants to live in a world without those? Not me(asle). These are the same scientists who say that having measles, mumps, or rubella is bad. And we know *that*'s not true. Some of my best friends are rubella viruses, and they are delights to be around. I think if you took the time to get to know rubella, you would see how wrong you are. (Mumps can be a drag, though. I'll give you that.)

Besides, you let chicken pox and the flu just ROAM FREE among you. You even have a season where you celebrate flu and pass it around to all your family members. And suddenly MEASLES is the villain here? Um, prejudice, much?

People are even saying that they don't want measles in Disneyland. Excuse me, but the last time I checked, Disneyland was a dreamworld of magic that welcomed EVERYONE, and your narrow-minded judgments have no place there. I've never been, myself, but it's on my bucket list. Frankly, I do not get out as much as I would like, having been contained in a glass vial until just recently.

Listen, the science on vaccination is very, very unsettled. Super unsettled. I bet if the Senate voted on the science of vaccinations right now, they would be about split down the middle. That's how unsettled it is. People who believe in vaccines probably think that Earth is more than 6,000 years old or that evolution is some kind of weird conspiracy, and, hey, I'm pretty sure there is room for discussion on both of those, and we should have a full debate. Debates are good. The more debates the better, I, a measles germ, say.

January 22, 2015

Sorry, I Obey the Billy Graham Rule

A wise Mississippi gubernatorial candidate refused to allow a female journalist to join him in his truck, on the grounds that he obeyed the Billy Graham Rule—a wise and correct prohibition on ever being alone at any time with a woman who is not your wife, whose necessity is explained below.

No! No! I CANNOT BE alone with a woman! Please! I beg of you!

Nothing will happen, of course. I hope. I pray. But please, let us not test it! My truck, my rules. I took a vow.

You do not know what I will become! You have not seen the horror that I struggle at all times to contain.

If you were in a situation where you had to move a cabbage, a fox, a woman, and myself across a river, I would beg you: Take them, take them and go! Leave me alone on the shore, where I can do no harm. Build a tower around me. Let thorny vines grow up all around it, until it is obscured from view. Forget the location of the tower. Burn all maps containing it. Then, only then, can women be truly safe.

Oh, this curse, this curse! I cannot bear it.

What I would give to look at a woman and see a person. I am told that is what others see. If only—if only—

You understand, I have this horrible condition. I have had it for years. I am incapable of seeing women as people. It used to be possible to get by in political life in this country with this condition. You would just move around a smoky room, speaking only to men, and you could have a nice career. But now, oh, these things, these things are everywhere. Holding elected office, performing jobs, playing soccer! You must understand my agony when I behold this. So much good meat, delicious meat, wonderful meat—

It is with difficulty that I shamble into the company of people every day. It is with difficulty that I convince people that I am, after all, a human being, not a wild animal, the mad, helpless victim of an uncontrollable lust. I cannot, I dare not—oh, it is with difficulty that I write these words now, knowing a woman may read them. The mere thought of my words moving before her unprotected eyes sends me into a frenzy. Fffffffft rrrrrrrrr graaarrrfll rrrrrr.

No women in the truck!

My truck is my sanctum sanctorum, my place of rest and quietness. But it is a struggle. Once a leaf landed on the window that looked like a woman's profile, and I had to brake abruptly. Someone left a file folder with suggestive curves on the passenger seat, and I nearly drove off the road. I saw a picture of Hillary Clinton on a roadside billboard and I had to pull over immediately. Such is my struggle. I am scarcely fit for human company.

If you know of anyone who can break this curse, oh, what a relief it would be. My wife, too, could be alone with people! We would both be free from this agony. But as it is, I am a wolf bundled in an ill-fitting button-down shirt. I am a wild beast.

I am a pestilence. Perhaps, in fact, I should not go out in public at all.

Do not let me out of the house! Or if I am so honored to be elected by you the people, the governor's mansion!

———————

July 11, 2019

I Am a State Legislator and I Am Here to Substitute-Teach Your Biology Class

HI KIDS! I'M A STATE LEGISLATOR—male, naturally—but really, at heart, I am an expert on the female body. You may know me from some of my work in Georgia, Alabama, and Ohio.

Ms. Roberts is out today, so I am here to cover the basics of reproductive anatomy. Which, again, I am expert in.

I am very excited to teach you about the reproductive system. We see here on this chart a body with a womb. The amazing thing about this body is that, unlike your body, which contains a person 100 percent of the time—you!—it only contains a person SOMETIMES.

One of the most common misconceptions people have about women, especially at your age, is that they are people. The idea that women are people is actually a relatively recent innovation, but my extensive knowledge of science—I once heard Ben Shapiro lecture!—reveals that actually they are vessels that may potentially contain people. Like a decorative fish tank, right after you have put the little diver in, but before there is water.

This is the womb. When a woman becomes hysterical, it wanders about the body. A woman is often hysterical, as when she shouts at you that this is not valid science. In such cases just say, "Lady-part, lady-part, fly away home!" and wait for it to return to its home (you will know that it has returned when she is finally, blessedly, silent). The womb is the only part of a woman that counts.

The female also possesses something that looks almost like a mouth, and something that looks almost like a brain, which some suggest it uses to attempt rudimentary communications; we have discovered writings and recordings made by females, but we have yet to decode them or, indeed, determine whether they make any sense at all. It is doubted by the Learned Scholars (in whose number I count myself) that they are decipherable at all.

This part—I don't know what this part is. It probably is not important to the woman, whose body is a big Pandora's box full of mysteries and ghosts. It looks sort of like a lung but I don't THINK girls have those—or if they do they are probably decorative pink lungs as opposed to the functional salmon-colored lungs possessed by men.

Very little is understood about what mechanism powers the woman. Steam? Coal? White wine? Humors? The important thing is that there is this—sort of—place for a baby, and amazingly, through some sort of miracle, beneath it are legs to help this empty vessel walk around on the land. And, proteins, I think?

So, uh. Processes. Ovulation is a very convoluted process which it is not necessary to understand. It takes no time, or perhaps a lot of time? Anyway, in this process the egg promenades lustfully along a stretch of uterus to see if she will catch the eye of any venturesome and praiseworthy sperm. It happens either monthly, annually, or never, and it makes women irrational and causes their sanguine humors to predominate, which is what gives them the ability to control the tides, become werewolves, and make cats their familiars.

The woman is full of eggs. This can be confusing. Where does the shell go? What does she do with the shell? Is that why she is always so upset when you try to explain to her how she is doing something wrong? Because there are little bits of shell inside her? Science cannot explain this.

The beginning of life is the result of two people performing a sacred act that is usually reserved for marriage, or if the president of the United States has become acquainted with an adult film performer and formed a special bond. Don't worry, the female body has ways of shutting the whole thing down. Or is that ducks? I might be thinking of ducks. It doesn't matter.

So uh you see here this sort of eggplant thing, that is . . . gross and we need not give it a name! Probably it is either the uterus, the cervix, fallopian tubes, or the clitoris?

The female body, like the Internet, is a series of tubes. Fallopian tubes are some tubes that are there; sometimes an egg will be careless and get itself fertilized in one of them because it has not been taking proper precautions (the egg ought to take precautions!), and in that case you can just kind of grab it and put it where it is supposed to go, but first you should give it a stern talking to. This is science, and we are trying to make it law, also.

The clitoris is like the Northwest Passage: Many men perished searching for it in vain; it does not exist, and never has. Do not go looking for it; you will surely die, and first you will have to see your dogs die.

This thing that looks sort of like a carrot that is having some problems is just—icky, and we need not discuss it, I think. It is a great mystery of the sort Man Was Not Meant to Know. It stores witchcraft and secrets and the ability to knit and perform emotional labor.

You might mistake this anatomy for a person, but actually it is just something that could contain a person; the moment the thingy is implanted in the whatsit by the you-know-what in a process that I fully understand—that is the moment there is a person. And the thing around it, that featherless biped which erroneously felt maybe that it was in possession of a soul—ceases to exist or to be of any interest to science. I am pretty sure. It can be discarded like a Whopper wrapper, to which, indeed, it is analogous—it is no longer important.

Again, these are not people. Indeed, as a special treat, I have brought one of these fantastic vessels for you to dissect and legislate upon to your heart's content today.

Do not worry. No matter what she says, it will not hurt her; she is not real like you.

May 11, 2019

Male Authors Describe Men in Literature Right

I am not alone in noticing that male authors sometimes fall short—that is, they spend so much of their ammunition in their glorious and perfect descriptions of female characters that they sometimes, I fear, do not take quite the same care with their men. Imagine if we lived in a world where they did! Well, you need imagine no longer. I have fixed it.

RAYMOND CHANDLER

Marlowe was the kind of brunette who would make a bishop kick a hole in a stained-glass window, and only half the hole would be from heterosexual panic. The other half would be that look he gave you, under his hat brim, the kind of look you thought you could cash in later in a cheap hotel room, before you saw the headache sticking out of his hip pocket.

LEO TOLSTOY

Vronsky had once been beautiful. His hands, once white and soft, were thin and wasted from the labors of child-rearing, and his face appeared pinched and unattractive. His voice had acquired a querulous tone. His arms, once the right shape, were now the wrong shape, because of the passage of time and the moral degradation that came with it. There was a horse who suffered an awful accident, and Vronsky was like that in a way.

HOMER

White-thighed Odysseus emerged from the water freshly
    bathed and glistening with oil
His skin glowed like the dawn sweeping in on his swiftly
    sandaled feet
The goddess beheld him with rapture

GEORGE R. R. MARTIN

Jon Snow's abs moved imperceptibly beneath his tunic, firm and hard and pale like winter apples that had been harvested, sliced carefully, and arrayed in rows.

JOHN UPDIKE

He peed, but he had no idea how, because inside his body was anatomy that was impossible to understand.

ERNEST HEMINGWAY

He had a butt that looked good. She grasped the butt with her hands. He was a bit put out but not too much. This was how things went between men and women.

JACK KEROUAC

His lovely ripe pectorals were barely concealed beneath his white nightshirt, and Dean looked at me as if to say, if this is America, I'd like to see more of it.

WILLIAM FAULKNER

He had been a big man once, but now his skeleton rose, draped loosely in unpadded skin that tightened again upon a paunch almost dropsical, as though muscle and tissue had been courage or fortitude which the days or the years had consumed until only the indomitable skeleton was left rising like a ruin or a landmark or a statue or a monument to a cause that boys see not once but whenever they want it, so it's always the instant when it's still not yet two o'clock on a July afternoon in 1863, the brigades in position behind the rail fence, the guns laid and ready in the woods and the furled flags already loosened, every year for a thousand years.

THE TERMINATOR

Large but delicately framed, with a pinprick red eye that lights up when he enters a room. He stops the party when he walks into a room (by killing the party with his mechanized weaponry), but you wonder what lurks under that steely exterior.

TOY STORY

Possessing a promising body with hard, shapely curves, Buzz dresses older than his age, but manages to pull it off.

PULP FICTION

With silky dark hair and full lips, Vincent is a Greek god. He walks and his shoes slap on the floor. His mane of lustrous black hair and his turtle neck (not turtleneck, that is something different) poke up out of a boxy suit, like a prairie dog saying hello.

FERRIS BUELLER'S DAY OFF

Ferris isn't the hottest guy in class, but he's definitely top five.

Star Wars: A New Hope
Luke Skywalker is in his late teens, pretty without knowing it.

Star Wars: The Empire Strikes Back
Darth Vader could be attractive if he tried, but he has instead settled for menacing. Tall, dressed in all black with a breathing mask affixed to his face—an outfit that screams, "LEAVE ME ALONE."

Lawrence of Arabia
Lawrence is strikingly beautiful with piercing blue eyes, but hides it in large, bulky garments.

E.T. the Extra-Terrestrial
With a lithe, lissome neck and large, expressive blue eyes, he looks damn good on a bicycle.

Jaws
Wearing nothing at all, the shark emerges from the water. We can't help but be fixated on this toothsome vision of beauty. Our eyes are drawn first to his mouth, large and sensuous, full of even, white teeth. But then they're drawn along his body's sleek curves—a body that throbs with raw sensuality and hunger, like an automobile that throbs with raw sensuality and hunger.

Raiders of the Lost Ark
Indiana Jones is in his thirties, but he's dressed like a much younger man in a half-unbuttoned shirt and a hat that he thinks too much of. He wears glasses, but would look good without them.

THE MUPPETS

With soft, peach-fuzz skin, Kermit the Frog intrudes on the viewer's attention not gradually but all at once. Unaware of his impact, and stronger than he knows.

2001: A SPACE ODYSSEY

The first thing you notice about HAL 9000, a glowing red boob in space, is that he's a glowing red boob in space.

April 4, 2018

Surprise! I'm Back,
and I Atoned

I'M BACK! I KNOW I admitted to doing some lousy things to women who trusted me and looked up to me. But don't worry. I atoned.

I did Whole30. I walked across a lake of fire. I listened to some podcasts where people did not hold back. I did sit-ups. I lived in a hut. In a hair shirt! By candlelight! For a year! Well, less than a year. And not by candlelight. Or in a hut. Or any of those other things. But for a period of literal months, I did not do something that I wanted to do. Which is an extremely long time.

So it turns out that nothing you do actually has any consequences. Have you noticed this? I always felt like if you did something really wrong you would be stopped somehow, and if no one stopped you, it couldn't be that wrong. Like, when your computer won't let you click on something. Ding! Not allowed! Or like a video game. "Sir, that's a wall. You're trying to walk through a wall." Oh, okay. Thank you, game, for looking out for me and not letting me walk through that wall. But if the game is like, obviously, it is *frowned* upon to drive the wrong way down the highway and murder the women you encounter, but, you know, we have programmed it so that if you want to, you *can*. That doesn't feel like it's on me! That feels like it's a programming failure on the game's part.

You know how if you leave a cat alone for three days with

a bag of food, the cat will figure out how much food it should eat and pace itself, but if you leave a dog alone for three days with a bag of food, the dog will just eat the entire bag of food because there is nothing there to stop them? I resemble that second thing. You want me to—not do this thing? But *nothing* will stop me? And afterward people will offer to clean up? That can't be right. This feels like a setup. I am offended. I think someone owes *me* an apology, frankly.

And if I did do a bad thing, can't I atone? Like in the old days. When you could go and do a series of labors and then they would be like, oh, didn't he murder his mother? No, yeah, he totally did, but he traveled a lot and then he touched the Shrine of Athena, so, it's, like, fine. You know? Didn't he light his spouse on fire? Yeah, but he went down to Hades and he walked this dog, and, so, you know, clean slate.

It doesn't seem fair that today if you do something bad, you're just—stuck. Like, you can literally make "Ignition (Remix)" and people are like, nope, still a bad person. And you're supposed to go away forever. Forever? That's like, multiple minutes. I'm just supposed to sit underground forever where no light shines, like some kind of albino mushroom or a woman's career?

I'm not denying that I did something that was wrong. I do understand that. I feel bad. I have felt bad! I felt really bad for a really long time! People yelled at me, and I had to sit there and listen to them tell me that I made them feel bad, and I felt bad. That is a terrible feeling. I don't want to overstate this, but I think it is literally the worst feeling in the world, having other people tell you that you did something wrong.

Although, are we 100 percent sure about this whole right and wrong thing? I'm just asking! I'm just putting it out there! Science, I feel like, science has figured life out, it knows about cells and things. But philosophy is just sort of like—we have some theories. No one's like, well, we've made a big breakthrough in philosophy, we've figured out definitely what is and is not moral to do, you know? Like, the ancient Greeks, they were maybe the best at philosophy, but to get to the philosophy you have to wade through like a whole framing device about courting a young boy. Before we reach the metaphysics, it is very urgent that I give you these tips for hitting on adolescents! Which doesn't make you feel *great* about philosophy, going in. So maybe there is no right or wrong! Maybe nothing I've done has any impact on anyone! In which case I have definitely put in enough time.

I want to do my task. I want to be like, I've atoned! I went down to Hades and I walked a dog, and I also slew this big beast with like eight heads, more heads all the time! I had to singe the necks! It was incredibly difficult! And then I put a microphone on my shoulder and I walked until nobody knew what it was, and I lived there for up to six entire weeks, so Poseidon isn't allowed to still be mad.

Everyone's like, why did you do that? Did you ask the people affected by your behavior what they wanted, and they said to do that? Did you read the suggestions that people came up with for what you could do to make this right? No, no, I just did the beast thing, because that is what you do to atone. I think we can agree that it was very difficult to do what I did with the beast and the dog, much more difficult than talking to the people I hurt, who are, for the most part, nice people who are easy to talk to. What I did was the harder thing. I decided that.

And I get that some things you should not be able to ever atone for. Not ever. Except, maybe? Maybe if the thing you do is really difficult? Like, if I got rid of malaria, just eradicated it completely, I feel like people shouldn't get to still be mad at me.

That's cutting off your not-having-malaria-as-a-species to spite your doing-bad-things guy. I think if you do something like get rid of malaria people should have to forgive you. I did not do that, but it's okay because I did the next best thing, which was nothing. For a few months. Which is like forever.

So, I atoned.

August 29, 2018

Without the Swimsuit Part of Miss America, When Will I Be Able to Judge Women's Appearances?

OH NO! I, A REASONABLE MAN, am devastated to learn there is no longer a swimsuit portion in the Miss America competition! And the evening-wear portion is now whatever the contestants want to wear, which could be anything at all, and which might be a bulky and functional tarpaulin that would delight my eyes not one whit!

This is egregious! If there is no bathing-suit competition, when can I hope to judge women on their appearance, except on dating apps,

or when they appear on television to talk about the lifesaving surgery they just performed on a pair of conjoined twins,

or when they are serving me at a Hooters restaurant,

or a regular restaurant,

or when they're bringing me a cup of cranberry-apple juice on an airplane,

or when they are applying for a job,

or when I am reading their scholarly research articles online and there isn't even a picture so I have to Google the name and cannot even be sure that the appearance of the person I am criticizing is the relevant person,

or when they make a YouTube video,

or when a man does something awful to them and they appear in court to testify about it,

or when they are running for office,

or when they are on television telling me the weather,

or when they are trying to ask a question during a news conference,

or when they are representing the country at the Olympics,

or when they are walking in front of me on the sidewalk,

or when they are my colleague,

or when I am suggesting that they reallocate their sexual resources in a rational manner (I suggest this completely dispassionately with no self-interest whatsoever, and I have devised a complex numerical system),

or when they perform music on national television,

or when they are engaging in activism to end gun violence,

or when they are the first lady or the former first lady,

or when they are in a Star Wars movie and I didn't like the Star Wars movie,

or when they are on the receiving end of sexual advances from the president,

or when they work for the president,

or when they work against the president,

or when they appear on the cover of magazines,

or when they write something and put it online and I had to squint at the avatar that was one inch by one inch and conclude, from this highly pixelated monstrosity, that I Would Not Bang,

or when they are on the radio, which takes real effort,

or when they wrote a novel in the eighteenth century,
or when they are a character in an ongoing fantasy epic,
or when someone wants to put them on currency,
or on Thursdays?

Except for these scant few contexts, I will have nothing! The swimsuit contest must be saved.

Already, this has gone too far.

June 5, 2018

I'm Fine with Women in Power, Just Not This One Specific Woman Currently in Power

THE FIRST THING I NEED to make clear is that I love and support women. I am eager to see more women rise to positions of power. Hashtag #pinkwave! Hashtag #pinkhat!

But I have to say, I'm a little frustrated that we keep putting forward this specific woman who really grinds my gears. Not because she's a woman. I would know if that was why. It is not that. It's just—ugh, *her*, you know? She just doesn't excite me, and I feel that she is too compromised. That's not a woman thing, though. It's just a *her* thing. I would have that issue with anyone who had her baggage, that same difficult-to-pin-down sense that something about her was fundamentally tainted.

But it is just this one woman in particular. And can I say how glad I am that we are at a point when we are able to judge women on their merits, as people, and find them inexplicably, inevitably wanting, as people? But definitely all women do not do this. There are plenty of women who do not make my teeth go on edge in the way this one lady does. My mother, for instance. My daughter, for another instance. And others I could name! Oprah, in her current capacity, though I hope she stays in her lane.

In general, I am excited to vote for a woman, maybe even in 2020, though I do, I have to say, worry that maybe other Americans are not so ready, and we wouldn't want to make that mistake in a year with such high stakes. Not me—I was born ready! I was given birth to by a woman. So it's clear where I stand.

That is why I am so frustrated with the specific women who keep being put forward. Like, Nancy Pelosi? I want women to lead everything! I want them to stare down charging bulls on Wall Street, and I can't imagine anyone other than a lady being Wonder Woman, but—this is the House we're talking about, and . . . ugh, Nancy Pelosi.

You see what I'm saying here. I am flabbergasted and upset that each and every one of the women being talked about as front-runners are the specific women who have already alienated me. I am as frustrated by this terrible coincidence as you are, believe me! Believe, women!

What I want is not impossible! I want someone who is not tainted by polarizing choices in the past, but who also has experience, who is knowledgeable but doesn't sound like she is lecturing, someone vibrant but not green, someone dignified but not dowdy, passionate but not a yeller, precise but not mechanical, someone lacking in off-putting ambition but capable of asking for what she wants, not accompanied but not alone, in a day but not in a month or a year, when the moon is neither waxing nor waning, carrying a sieve full of water and a hen's tooth. Easy!

That's why I'm so worried about our current slate of choices. A woman, sure, but—Kamala Harris? Elizabeth Warren? Kirsten Gillibrand? There are specific problems with each of them, entirely personal to each of them, all insurmountable. We need someone fresh. Someone without baggage. Joe Biden, maybe. But female! If you see.

I can't wait to vote for a woman in 2020. A nameless, shapeless, faceless woman I know nothing about who will surely be perfect.

November 18, 2018

I Am in Favor of Confederate Statues. I Am Definitely Not a Pigeon.

TWO REASONS I AM DEFINITELY not here protesting the removal of this Confederate statue: because I am a white supremacist who wants to protect a racist legacy, or because I am a pigeon who has laid an egg on this statue somewhere.

Listen, like you, I am a human being. I have zero feathers but many gangly appendages covered in skin, and I am flightless. Yet in spite of this, I love these statues, and not because their little metal hats are great places in which to build a foundation of carefully selected twigs, twine, and assorted debris, then lay a warm, beautiful egg that will someday hatch into a magnificent, glorious bird, the king of the air.

I am one of the "very fine people" whom President Trump was talking about, definitely a person, who was there to protest the taking down of the statue for human reasons that had nothing to do with racism or the nest of vulnerable white eggs currently exposed in that Confederate general's hat.

I am a human being like you, a featherless biped with hairs all over my epidermis. And I am not a racist. I don't know what the word "racism" means. Also, I don't see color. I perceive light on the ultraviolet spectrum. As everyone here does, I hope. That is how we humans perceive light, I am pretty sure.

Getting rid of these statues would be for the birds, an expression I use in its derogatory sense, as we humans often do.

Like so many of us here, I do not have a racist bone in my body, though if I did that racist bone would *definitely* be dense and not hollow. I just want to protect my nest egg—NOT a literal egg in a nest, of course, but one of those metaphorical nest eggs we human beings are always so upset about. Economic anxiety? Yes, I have that. That is what I have. My nest egg, again, is metaphorical, not literally on this statue right now, vulnerable and exposed with its white shell open to the elements. KEEP THAT TORCH AWAY from what is definitely not my only genetic legacy, but a beautifully constructed nest that is unaffiliated with me, a human protester.

This is a normal request from me, a human, perched here with you in solidarity on my two appendages. I am not here to fan the flames of hatred, an action that I would do with hands and not wings, obviously. I am not a hawk, nor a dove. I am not a bird at all, again. I am not affiliated with any sort of organization with "coo" or "clucks" in its name, neither for racist reasons *nor* for the reason that these are noises a bird would make. I distance myself from both of those things equally.

Like so many of you, when I look at this statue, I do not see a figure of hate. I don't see a figure at all, honestly. More of a blur. And that is not because I am viewing it from above while soaring aloft on the wings that are the greatest boon that can be bestowed by nature, but for another reason that I do not need to spell out.

Like all of you, I just want to keep this statue here for reasons that do not have anything to do with wanting to defecate on it, lay eggs on it, or perch on it to preen my beautiful gray feathers. Or, of course, racism. Those are just a few of the MULTIPLE reasons that I do not have for wanting this statue to stay exactly where it is, conveniently located near a man on a bench who often eats french fries—a fellow man, I should say, a fellow very fine being who has hideous bone protrusions at the opening to his alimentary canal that he uses to masticate food, just as I do.

This isn't a pigeon issue. This statue doesn't provide succor to just racists and pigeons. Who among us has not sheltered here during a high wind and enjoyed a french fry he or she found on the sidewalk and lifted with great effort?

I don't think anyone seeing this statue would reasonably think, "I am not welcome here." Unlike other statues that carry boom boxes and move and demand money and raise their hideous featherless wings to strike at those good citizens who would land on them, these statues are peaceful and quiet. They are just CRYING OUT to be perched on, either by humans, like myself, or sparrows, whom I spite as good-for-nothings.

It is, to me, as Trump says (not tweets—I, a human, would not understand a tweet), a very, very important statue. I am a human person, very fine, and I am not here because of racism. I just want to protect that statue, at all costs.

Yes, I am a hardworking American who struggles all day and then goes home to vomit food into my children's mouths, and I am sick to see what we are doing to this absolutely nonpolarizing landmark.

Please don't photograph me—not because I am ashamed to be here (because I am NOT) or because, if there is a flash, I will fly up into the sky in great alarm (I will not do that EITHER, defi-

nitely). I just do not like photos—AAAAAH OH GOD FLAP
FLAP FLAP FLAP GET AWAY GET AWAY.

Okay, you got me—I am a pigeon. I am not sure what these
people are doing.

_____

August 17, 2017

Coda

YOU MAY THINK THAT YOU are at the end of this book, but I assure you, you are not. This is not the end, but the beginning. If the book appears to be running out of words, that just shows your own lack of imagination, and I am very sorry for you. This is a signal that your mind is faulty, and you ought to go back to the beginning and read very carefully from there until you reach this point again and see how mistaken you were. You are not at the end yet. This book has no end. Ignore the evidence of your eyes and ears, if they are attempting to tell you otherwise. Trust only to my voice.

I have saved the most beautiful words for the end. They are extremely numerous and extremely beautiful, but only the pure of mind may read them.

Here they are:

If you cannot read them, that is because your mind is not yet pure enough. Clear your mind and try again. Forget a little algebra. Forget anything you know about carbon sequestration, certainly. Absolutely forget the Constitution. You should have forgotten it long ago. Keep trying for those words. You will be sure to see them, and they will be absolutely perfect.

Do not read any other books that would tell you that anything in here was not, strictly speaking, correct. Those books have their own agendas. Keep the door of your mind firmly shut against them. If you allow the door to open even a crack, monsters will get in. Or light, or something worse. It is much better to stay here, where it is safe, where you will see how right I was to warn you.

Keep looking!

They are here and they are beautiful. When you see them, you will clap.

We are not monsters, you and I.

ACKNOWLEDGMENTS

EVERY DAY I AM FLABBERGASTED and delighted that I get to work at the *Washington Post*. Enormous thanks and the most effusive of acknowledgments to Fred Hiatt—without whom, nothing!—for all your kindness and encouragement since my intern days, and for making this book possible, both in the direct causal sense and in the proximate causal sense. Thank you also to all the wonderful folks who have edited me along the way—especially Ruth, Molly, and Drew—for turning things that were unintelligible ALL CAPS into things that were legible and even publishable. And a big thank you also to Richard Aldacushion at the Post Writers' Group.

Massive thanks to my indefatigable, luminous agent Anna. And violent appreciation to my editor Tom and the team at Norton who have shepherded this to publication.

Thank you to everyone who puts up with me on a regular basis: Steve, my parents, my grandmother and extended family, JGolds, the Food Brigade, the Strombergs, and the cast and creative team of the Terror. This is for you!

And Madeleine, always.